REPEAT BUSINESS INC

The Business of Staying in Business

RESEAT
BUSINESS

The science of
doing business

REPEAT BUSINESS INC

The Business of Staying in Business

50 Tips and Strategies You Can Do Today to Keep Your Customers Coming Back Tomorrow

PAUL RUTTER

Copyright © 2017 by Paul Rutter

All rights reserved. No part of this book may be used or reproduced in any manner whatsoever without prior written consent of the author, except as provided by the United States of America copyright law.

Printed in the United States of America.

ISBN-13: 978-1542637817 ISBN-10: 1542637813

Smooth Sailing Communication, Inc. is a leading organization providing educational tools to help businesses exceed customer expectations with the **More Than Perfect®** Customer Service Model.

*For Jan, Lucy and Ricky, my wonderful support team that
helped immeasurably in so many ways.
To The Keynote Group for tremendous guidance and encouragement.
To Julia for her words of wisdom.
Thank you all from the bottom of my heart.*

TABLE OF CONTENTS

Introduction 1

SECTION I:
WHY CUSTOMER SERVICE IS GOOD FOR YOUR BUSINESS

1. Great Customer Service Increases Market Share 5
2. Great Customer Service Increases Customer Loyalty 9
3. It Costs Less to Keep Your Customers 13
4. Great Customer Service Increases Employee Loyalty 17
5. Great Customer Service Encourages New Ideas and Innovation ... 21
6. Great Customer Service Encourages Community Involvement 25
7. A Reputation for Great Service is Worth its Weight in Gold 29
8. Great Customer Service Builds Credibility and Trust 33
9. Great Customer Service Gives You a Competitive Edge 37
10. Resolving a Customer Service Issue Successfully
    Will Create Advocates for Your Company 41
11. Great Customer Service Improves Your Online Ratings 45
12. Great Customer Service Increases Your Company's Bottom Line .. 49

SECTION II:
WHAT YOUR CUSTOMERS WANT

13. Proactive Communication 55
14. Respect 59
15. To Have Their Problems Taken Seriously 63
16. To be Served Promptly 67
17. To Be Listened To 71
18. Prompt Attention to a Complaint or Concern 75
19. Restitution for Time and Effort 77
20. To Feel Valued More than the New Customers You are Pursuing .. 81
21. Good Value 83
22. An Honest Deal 85
23. Rewards for Loyalty 87
24. Consistency 89

SECTION III:
WHAT YOUR EMPLOYEES NEED TO PROVIDE MORE THAN PERFECT CUSTOMER SERVICE

25. Communication Skills 95
26. Empathy 99
27. An Eye for Safety and Security 103
28. An Eye for First Impressions and Attention to Detail 107
29. The Authority to Solve Problems 111
30. Accountability 115
31. A Proactive but Flexible Approach 119
32. A Positive Attitude 123
33. A Desire to Learn 127
34. The Ability to Set Reasonable and Clear Customer Expectations . 131
35. The Desire to Connect Personally with Customers 135

SECTION IV:
WHAT YOU NEED TO LEAD A COMPANY THAT GIVES MORE THAN PERFECT SERVICE

36. Strong Role Models 141
37. Respect for the Power of Choice 145
38. High Standards 149
39. Determination 153
40. Three Key Attributes: Respect, Responsibility and Reliability 157
41. Three Important Values: Empathy, Gratitude and Compassion ... 161
42. A Strong Plan 165
43. Optimism 169
44. Availability 173
45. A Good Sense of Humor 177
46. A Healthy Body 179
47. Genuine Interest in Your Customers and Coworkers 183
48. Cultural Intelligence 187
49. A Commitment to Make "Uncommon Courtesy" Common 191
50. Comfort with Change 195

Conclusion 198

INTRODUCTION

A few years ago, a man named Yasser took me and some of my family members on a full day tour of the Egyptian Pyramids. The day had been unforgettable. He had timed each event—from our meals to our camel ride to our time up close and personal with the pyramids themselves—to ensure that we avoided the thousands of tourists that tend to make such tours feel like a cattle call.

It was as if we had this extraordinary treasure of the ancient world all to ourselves. As an Egyptologist, he regaled us with the backstory of each monument, translating hieroglyphics and transporting us in our imaginations back thousands of years. Later, I would describe the experience he gave us as "more than perfect."

Customer service has never been more important than it is today. Not long ago, you would walk to the corner market and speak personally with your butcher to order what you needed for the week. He gave everyone who shopped there personal service, and they trusted him. He didn't have to do much marketing, because all his customers were local. Yet sometimes in such a trusting community environment, a snake oil salesman could go from town to town, cheating people out of their money for years before word of mouth caught up with him.

Today, the internet allows us to buy from all over the world, as well as read about others' experiences with products and services we are considering. This has changed customer service in ways that no one could have anticipated. First of all, customers are often more educated than in the past. Instead of subscribing to the print edition of a consumer reports magazine, they can look up hundreds of customer reviews on their smartphones. Not only that, but customers can (and will!) tell their hundreds of Facebook friends or thousands of Twitter followers about the positive or negative experiences they've had with your business.

Yet most businesses are not rising to this new challenge. Despite thousands of expensive initiatives and campaigns, a 2013 survey conducted by Customer Care Measurement and Consulting in conjunction with Arizona State University found that Americans are more dissatisfied than ever with the products and services they buy and with the customer service they receive when they complain. At least 56 million households had a negative experience with a purchase in the last year, jeopardizing over 76 billion dollars in revenue for the businesses involved.

Consumers are living in a world of paradoxes. They may choose to live in immense, bustling cities, but they long for the sense of community and the personal touch found in small towns. They can buy their goods and services with the click of a button, but their purchase experiences can be as frustrating as trying to get a three year old to sleep after being pumped full of sugar at Grandma's house. They fork over billions of dollars to giant corporations on a daily basis, yet they're convinced that those companies don't care about them at all.

After years of successfully cultivating repeat business in the hospitality industry, I've learned that the companies that win in today's business environment are the ones that learn to forge meaningful, personal connections with their customers. Like my now good friend Yasser, they offer service that is more than perfect, because it is personal. This book will explain why you must prioritize this kind of service, what your customers are looking for, what your employees need and lastly what you need—as a leader—to keep your customers coming back over and over again.

SECTION I

WHY CUSTOMER SERVICE IS GOOD FOR YOUR BUSINESS

We all know that customer service is important, just like we know it's important to eat our vegetables and exercise regularly. But if knowledge alone did the trick, we'd all be wearing the same size pants we wore back in high school (which I can do if I only put in one leg). Knowing customer service is important does not mean we are doing all the little things on a daily basis that will ensure our customers keep coming back to us over and over. Specifically, we must treat customer service as essential to our businesses' survival, both in the short term and in the long term.

Have you ever heard someone explain a divorce as the result of "a lot of little things"? In the hustle and bustle of daily life, it can be so easy to neglect the little displays of care and affection that make a marriage work. The same is true of the customer-business relationship. If we don't focus on the specific cause and effect relationship between good customer service and a better bottom line, it becomes very easy for the little details that should nurture that relationship to get lost in the shuffle.

Building customer relationships takes time, effort and authentic care, just as building a successful marriage takes dedication, selflessness and daily apologizing (if you're the Husband). Much like your marriage, once you do build a solid relationship with a customer, the return on that investment is greater than you can imagine. For example, a popular family-owned restaurant in Worcester, Massachusetts learned that it needed $50,000 worth of renovations to bring its kitchen up to code. Restaurants typically operate on razor-thin profit margins—particularly when catering to a student population as they did—and they did not have enough cash in reserve to cover the needed repairs. The mother and daughter who owned the restaurant had worked tirelessly for years to make sure their customers were always satisfied, had earned their reputation as a place where students were treated with respect, had become a beloved part of the local community, and were saddened by their certainty that they would have to close.

When their customers learned of the situation, the restaurant owners were in for a shock. Rather than just coming in to have one last dinner as the establishment prepared to close, the customers rallied to its aid. A crowd funding account had soon raised more than two thirds of the needed balance, and the nearby university offered an interest free loan to cover the rest. The restaurant's more than perfect customer service and experience literally saved its business.

But you don't need to be facing a crisis for customer service to affect your survival. Here are some simple facts about great customer service that will help you keep it at the top of your priority list:

GREAT CUSTOMER SERVICE INCREASES MARKET SHARE

Given the choice, customers would much rather be given superior customer service when making their purchases. Social media and online consumer report lists make it incredibly easy for customers to compare not only the quality of a product or service, but also the experience of the purchase. And if customers were unhappy with how they were treated or how a complaint was handled, you can bet everyone is going to hear about it.

According to the 2012 Global Customer Service Barometer (conducted by Echo Research for American Express), customers are twice as likely to talk about a bad customer service experience as they are to talk about a positive one. At face value, this might seem to indicate that you have a lot more to lose with customer interactions than you have to gain. But think of that first interaction with a new customer like a first date: even the most magical first date with candlelight and a carriage ride probably won't persuade her to marry you, but a terrible time of going dutch at the WallyBurger drive-thru will certainly convince her that she never wants to see you again!

Negative social media buzz about your business can take on many forms. Someone may tweet or post something vague like "Never going to [Your Business] again!" to invite their followers to ask what happened. Or they may post a full length rant offering every frustrating detail of the experience. Either way, a momentary decision on the part of a dissatisfied customer can dissuade countless potential customers from ever even giving you a try. This means that making customer service a priority can help ensure you don't lose potential customers before you even meet them. Think of it this way: if she tells her friends about the WallyBurger date, odds are pretty good none of them are going to spend an upcoming Saturday night with you!

Conversely, if people have a good experience with your company they are more likely to recommend you to their friends and family members. Furthermore, such referrals start building trust with new customers before they even interact with you directly. Even better, the word of mouth referrals that come from satisfied customers don't cost you anything and are usually more effective than pricier forms of advertising.

In fact, companies like Chick-fil-A that have prioritized more than perfect customer service (and product quality) over rapid expansion find themselves continuing to add stores, even in a struggling economy. In 2014, Yahoo Finance reported that Chick-fil-A had overtaken Kentucky Fried Chicken as the leading chicken fast food restaurant chain in America. The company, known for its consistently friendly and polite employees, did a larger volume of business than KFC, despite operating fewer locations and being closed one day a week. In contrast, in 2015 McDonald's closed more US restaurant locations than it opened.

As market share increases, customer service becomes even more vital. Many businesses see their customer satisfaction rates drop as their customer base grows, and this can occur for several reasons. Sometimes new employees are added to keep up with demand but the company lacks a thorough and effective customer service training program to ensure that their new employees will maintain the high quality their customers have come to expect.

Later in the book, we'll examine in more detail the companies that have grown successfully without compromising their high quality customer service.

REPEAT BUSINESS CHALLENGE

Gather your team and evaluate your entire customer experience. Discuss in detail these issues:
Can your customers easily connect with you?
- How easy is it to navigate your website?
- How long does it take your business to answer an email, or return a phone call?
- What is your return policy?
- What is your discovery process?
- How do you follow up with them to ensure repeat business?

Put a plan in motion that improves on these processes and provide regular feedback. It's critical to consistently and honestly evaluate these measures to ensure a great experience. The entire Customer Experience, from start to finish, will determine if they do business with you again.

GREAT CUSTOMER SERVICE INCREASES CUSTOMER LOYALTY

First we have to start with the negative: bad customer service almost always causes customers to leave. According to a recent Customer Experience Report by RightNow Technologies—a leading developer of Customer Relationship Management (CRM) software—the primary reason customers leave one company and go to a competitor is rude or poor customer service. This means that far more customers leave because of poor customer service than leave because a competitor has lower prices or faster service.

Why is this? Aren't we wired to do cost-benefit analyses of every transaction and act in our own economic self-interest? While price and quality will always be important factors in any purchase, poor customer service cuts into a different, much deeper human need: our need for respect. To wit: most of us are willing to pay a little bit more to be treated like an actual human being.

Rude customer service does more than annoy us: it communicates to us that we are not valuable to the company. In fact, according to the same report, 68 percent of customers left because they felt that the company did not care about them. Smile. Make eye contact. Say hello, please, and thank you. These are all free, fun, they don't promote tooth decay, and most importantly will make your customers feel important and persuade them to return. In a world where consumers have more choices than ever before, why would any company allow their customers to feel that they don't matter?

There are many reasons why businesses of all sizes let poor customer service slip through the cracks. Many business leaders assume that if they are not hearing a lot of complaints, their customers must be happy and their customer service must be great. In fact, multiple studies show that the average business hears from only a tiny percentage of its dissatisfied customers (most estimate around 4 percent).

Then there are the poorly trained customer service representatives. In a story that generated the worst possible publicity, a Comcast customer service representative famously refused to cancel the cable service for a 66 year old Jimmy Ware of St. Paul whose house burned down in a tragic fire. The representative claimed not to be able to cancel the service because he could not locate his account number.

Perhaps there were incentives in place to punish a representative from contacting a supervisor who might have been able to help. Perhaps it was this representative's first week on the job and he panicked. Perhaps it was almost lunch time and he was anxious to get to a date at WallyBurger. Perhaps he had a sociopathic lack of empathy and was big jerk - we don't know. What's most likely though, is that this individual was simply not trained to handle an emergency situation. Plenty of other huge firms with ample resources to train their employees fail to anticipate their customers' needs sufficiently. They treat the customer as a revenue source not a person. No matter the reason, the result of this situation was a deeply insulted customer and a public relations nightmare for Comcast.

On the other hand, customers who feel respected and valued are much more likely to be understanding when things don't go perfectly. Even if the Comcast representative hadn't known how to cancel the service, if he or she had at least expressed concern and sympathy for Ware's situation, it would have gone a long way toward diffusing what became a national embarrassment for the company.

REPEAT BUSINESS CHALLENGE

Sit down with your team and have an open dialogue regarding areas of improvement and how you can obtain customer feedback. Some potential ways to obtain customer feedback:

- Create a survey where customers can evaluate your service.
- Encourage feedback online and when their invoice is delivered.
- Make a personal phone call to follow up with your customer and create a relationship with them that will lead to repeat business.

Increase your customer loyalty today by making it a personal experience for your customers. Respect for your customers is the key to loyalty and long-term success.

IT COSTS LESS TO KEEP YOUR CUSTOMERS

If you want to stay in business, you need to hang on to the customers you already have. This is a well-known fact, but it bears repeating: according to multiple studies, including one performed recently by the Lee Resource Group, Inc., it's 6-7 times more expensive to attract a new customer than it is to keep an existing one. Depending on the industry, keeping an existing customer can be as much as 21 times cheaper than attracting a new customer. In industries with longer sales cycles—where clients must be cultivated for months or even years before they buy—the cost of losing a customer is almost too large to calculate.

There are a lot of people in the world and it can be tempting to think that you can just go find more customers if your attrition rate starts to creep up. But swapping out an existing customer for a new one, or even two new ones, is not an even trade. According to Bain and Company, a global management consulting firm, just a 5 percent increase in customer retention can increase a company's profitability by 75 percent.

There are many causes of customer attrition in business, some of which are quite complicated and do not appear to be directly related to customer service. New products or services pop up all the time, and some of them will affect your industry. Customers' needs and behaviors change all the time too. At first glance, these issues would appear to be beyond the company's control. But well trained customer service representatives can constantly gather data on industry trends and customer needs during their daily interactions. The savvy business owner can use customer service expertise to keep the company abreast of any important shifts or changes.

Other causes of attrition are obviously customer service related. Besides the usual bad customer experience or the unresolved complaint, some customers leave a company because they feel they do not get consistent answers about a company policy for warranty, returns or discounts. Others may abandon you because another company makes them feel more valued. They may not have had a negative experience with you, but if someone else can give them a better experience, they are likely to leave. It's simple: if another company shows them candlelight and carriage rides while you continue to push WallyBurger, you'll be spending Saturday nights looking at an empty store and wondering why all the songs on the radio remind you of your lost customer.

The value of keeping your existing customers—while still working to win over new ones—becomes clearer when you think about the cost and effort of cultivating relationships. After all, you don't think casually about getting rid of old friends and finding new ones. It takes time and effort to build trust and bond with someone.

That's why you don't ask the guy you met at the gym last week to help you move. Helping with a move is reserved for the friends you've known since college, and who will work for beer and pizza. The cost of helping you move - beer and pizza - is close to nothing, but you only gain that return after putting in years of dedication to the friendship. Think of it this way - would you throw a little beer and pizza to your customers if you knew they'd come back, year after year? Of course you would.

Your customer service is ultimately about nurturing your relationships with your customers, and it is the most vital part of your customer retention program. If you don't do your best to provide an outstanding customer experience from day one—and deal effectively with the problems and imperfections that naturally come up—all the follow up marketing in the world will not keep your customers coming back. This is even truer of product driven businesses where there is little direct interaction with the customer. Just enclosing a note with the product when it arrives to thank the customer for the purchase or having a representative call personally to find out if the customer was satisfied can go a long way to cultivating the kind of loyalty that will keep you in business for a long, long time.

REPEAT BUSINESS CHALLENGE

Sit down with your team and come up with ways of letting your customers know how important they are to you and your business. It does not have to cost very much. A hand written *Thank You* note is remembered long after the sale is closed. Commit to implementing one new idea a month and monitor your increase in repeat business. You'll be shocked at how true the phrase "a little goes a long way" becomes!

GREAT CUSTOMER SERVICE INCREASES EMPLOYEE LOYALTY

"Kathy" arrived for her job interview ten minutes early. The position was for a customer service call center for a large electronics company. Her kids were just starting school, and she wanted to make some extra money working at a part time job. With a college degree, professional tone and a pleasant disposition, Kathy was an ideal customer service representative for the company. The person who interviewed her recognized this right away, and she was hired.

On Kathy's first day she was handed a thin manual with scripts for how to respond to the various scenarios she was likely to encounter. Unfortunately, she had no authority to fix any of the problems her customers were likely to have. Her main function was to try to discourage customers from returning faulty products. She was also given a bonus if she could persuade a customer to take store credit instead of cash for a return. After a couple of weeks on the job, she learned that refund checks promised to her customers took weeks or even months to arrive.

Kathy knew about multiple customer problems and grievances with her company, but she was completely powerless to do anything about them. Soon she began to dread going to work; she felt exhausted afterwards and found herself getting impatient with her children when they arrived home from school in the afternoon. After Kathy cashed her third paycheck, she quit. The money she was making was not worth the toll on her quality of life that her job was taking.

People like to feel competent at their jobs and proud of where they work. This is particularly true when they are the ones who are interacting directly with customers. When customers ask questions or make accusations for which they don't have a good answer, they feel frustrated and disempowered. And no one likes to be in a situation where they are forced to improvise an answer or make excuses for the sake of a company that doesn't seem to care.

You want your employees to work for you because they enjoy coming to work and believe in the quality of the product or service you provide. If they think the company is only using them to shield the leadership from legitimate complaints it does not intend to resolve, they will not feel obligated to care about the company's long term wellbeing. Remember, your employees are often a great source of insight into how to better serve your customers. If you don't make it clear that you care about providing excellent customer service, they will have no reason to bring you any ideas or insights they might have, and remember: the folks on "the front lines" often have a valuable understanding into the customer's mindset.

Loyal employees are also key to staying in business. Employee turnover is extremely costly: you must factor in recruiting, onboarding, training, as well as lost productivity, sales and temporary employee salary while you find someone permanent. This can cost anywhere from 150 percent to 250 percent of the employee's salary. In some industries, when a salesperson leaves, the company will lose any deals he or she had in the pipeline, as well as his or her relationships with clients and potential clients.

Ultimately, poor customer service and employee turnover become a vicious cycle. When Kathy left, there was no one to fill her place right away, which meant that customers had to be shifted to other employees who were already overburdened. Her replacement was not as qualified or professional as she was, and once he was hired he still had to be trained and took longer to learn how to handle Kathy's old duties. Ultimately, someone who is perfectly happy to NOT be able to help your customers isn't a person you want as an employee.

It is almost impossible to imagine a company that does not care about its customers but cares deeply about its employees. Caring about your customers is not something that happens in an emotional vacuum. You care about your customers because you value people and you have a sense of pride in the product or service you provide for them. When that is truly how you operate, you will attract and retain the best employees as well.

REPEAT BUSINESS CHALLENGE

Discuss with your team successful situations where they have displayed exceptional customer service and reward them with the trust and resources to handle certain customer concerns on the spot. Each month, let them share their experience and how they resolved it to encourage and empower others who have shown leadership qualities. Give them a reason to feel good about coming to work. It may cost a bit more in the short term, but long term you will gain loyalty from your customers as well as your employees.

GREAT CUSTOMER SERVICE ENCOURAGES NEW IDEAS AND INNOVATION

We tend to imagine new and innovative ideas coming from the minds of great inventors and engineers or from closed-door brainstorming sessions of high level executives. But in reality, when you have cultivated an environment of caring for people in your company, all your employees will look for ways to improve your product or service, as well as your overall production and delivery processes. In fact most great products and services are the result of a rich interaction between engineers, marketing experts and customers.

The role customer service plays in this process cannot be overstated. If you are not hearing from your customers on a regular basis, you will not really know what is working for them and what is not. You will not have a good sense of how their needs may be changing, and how your business may need to change to meet them. George Day, a professor of marketing at Wharton Business School at the University of Pennsylvania, explained the disconnect that can develop when company leaders do not get regular feedback from their customers:

> *"I think the biggest problems occur when you get strongly engineering-driven companies that don't really appreciate the emotional attachment people have to products or their emotional reactions to them, and think it's all about very specific product attributes."*

When customer feedback is not a major factor driving innovation, it is extremely easy for the process to go off track very quickly. Remember, not every new idea is going to lead to a successful new product roll out. Some will fail because of cost or other development logistics, but most will fail because they aren't successfully brought to market. What better way to ensure a higher percentage of your new ideas are successful than to let your customers' needs and values drive your innovation? Basically, it does not matter how awesomely fantastic YOU think your product is, it only matters what YOUR CUSTOMERS think - if you believe you're serving steak but you never hear that they think it's a WallyBurger, they will quickly stop coming back.

Perhaps the most famous example of the company—customer disconnect was the disastrous roll out of New Coke in 1985. Company leaders were shocked at the hostile reaction from customers to the change in the decades old soft-drink formula. They received over 400,000 letters and calls complaining about the change. Even though they had done all the market research and had impeccable reasoning behind the decision, they completely misunderstood the devotion of their best customers to the original formula.

When you make the effort to get to know your customers in a more holistic way, you will be able to innovate in ways that will be meaningful to them. For example, some of Royal Caribbean International's employees noticed that their customers were interacting on a particular website designed for reviewing cruises. They shared what they liked about each cruise. They shared what they did not like about each cruise. (They also shared pictures of themselves in Speedos, but that helped no one and isn't relevant to our discussion here.) Not only were the customers sharing their experiences on the site, but they were also beginning to plan their cruises to coincide with one another's. In response to the spontaneous development of this online community, Royal Caribbean began offering "Meet and Mingle" sessions for their guests who knew one another through these online forums. The customers greatly enjoyed the opportunity to get together and responded by promoting the Royal Caribbean brand to their friends and family members. Listening = repeat customers.

Some businesses find creative ways to engage customer feedback as they inspire their employees to innovate. Bars may hold a contest for their bartenders to create new drinks, allowing customers to sample them and vote for the winner. The contest itself generates brand interest and cultivates community, while the winning employee takes home a meaningful prize. Other companies offer significant cash awards for safety or other innovative suggestions that are adopted by the company.

The only way to know what your customers need is to interact with them. Training your employees to develop strong relationships with your customers offers you invaluable insight into what they want and need. It gives you more than just data points and answers on a survey; it gives you a complete picture of your customers as human beings.

REPEAT BUSINESS CHALLENGE

Conduct a monthly meeting where team members are encouraged to share ideas with management. Encourage all employees, especially those working directly with customers on the front line, to offer new ideas and suggestions based on their feedback and experiences. Offer incentives. You never know where the next great idea will come from.

GREAT CUSTOMER SERVICE ENCOURAGES COMMUNITY INVOLVEMENT

When you are truly connected to your customer base, you will have insight into the needs not just of individuals but also of the entire community they inhabit. In fact, a company's community involvement is an increasingly vital part of marketing and maintaining a positive brand image. According to a 2013 study by Cone Communications and Echo Research, 82 percent of consumers consider corporate social responsibility when what to buy and where to shop.

Furthermore, according to a Golin Harris study, employees' view of their company's corporate responsibility has a deep impact on company morale. Good people like working for a company they can be proud of. Younger workers in particular want to find meaning in the work they do, and they can if you make it clear that your company is helping to make the community it serves a better place.

There are countless opportunities to get involved. If your customer base has a lot of young families, you may want to sponsor some local sports teams or do something with the schools. If you serve a lot of retirees, you may sponsor gatherings or fitness events. Many businesses support causes by having certain time frames where a percentage of the profits go toward that cause. Others sponsor races or other community events to benefit disease research or a local institution such as the library, hospital or school. Larger businesses may want to adopt a larger charity that gives them a national or even international reach.

Never underestimate the power of being involved with the communities were your customers live. One local restaurant owner in Maryland decided on a whim to sponsor the summer swim team from a neighborhood in walking distance of his establishment. To show its gratitude, the team—which included over eighty swimmers and their families—decided to patronize his establishment one evening. The owner was shocked to realize that the increase in his profits from that single evening were more than the amount he had donated to the team. Not only that, most of the families had never eaten there before, so he had been given a great opportunity to welcome and serve new customers. (No, this restaurant was not called WallyBurger.)

There is a big difference between simply cutting a check for a good cause and having a meaningful impact on a community. When done correctly, community involvement is simply a natural outworking of your growing relationship with your customers. The more meaningful those relationships, the more meaningful your service efforts will be.

REPEAT BUSINESS CHALLENGE

Find at least one way your business can be involved in the community. Encourage and reward employees who get involved in the selected cause. The return you receive on employee morale, positive public perception, and free publicity will be incalculable.

A REPUTATION FOR GREAT SERVICE IS WORTH ITS WEIGHT IN GOLD

You may need a sound plan to get your business off the ground, but you need a stellar reputation to stay in business. According to a 2011 American Express Survey, 3 in 5 Americans (59 percent) said they would try a new brand or company in order to have a better service experience. Perhaps even more startling, 7 in 10 Americans said they were willing to spend more with companies they believe provide excellent customer service. So how do these consumers decide who will give them a better customer service experience? Much like the friends of the girl you had one date with, they rely on what they hear about you from people they trust - it's all about your reputation.

Your reputation is what people know about you and your company before they interact with you directly. It lays the groundwork for the relationships you will establish with your customers. Reputation not only helps determine which people will walk through your doors in the first place; it also shapes their expectations when they get there. Many times, a good reputation can make the difference between a customer who comes in with a sunny attitude and one who just tries to get out of your establishment as soon as possible.

Depending on your industry, potential customers may find selecting a product or service a tiresome process. All of us need repair technicians, cell phones and car insurance, but we don't want to spend hours researching our options. A reputation for great customer service cuts through the decision making process and encourages individuals to give you a try.

Of course staying in business sometimes means cutting costs. When there is a slowdown in an industry, a community or in the economy in general, it can be very important to reduce spending wherever possible. However, it is never wise to cut corners when it comes to the quality of your customer service. Maintaining a stellar reputation for customer service is actually your best bet for retaining as many of your customers as possible, even during a slowdown.

Ultimately, good customer service makes people want to do business with you. We've all bought cookies, candy or wrapping paper from the child of a relative or neighbor, not because we needed it, but because of our relationship with the seller. How much more will your customers want to buy from you if you are selling them something they actually need and you show them that you really do care?

REPEAT BUSINESS CHALLENGE

Do everything in your power to make sure your reputation stays at the highest level. Consistent feedback is essential in monitoring customer loyalty and brand reputation. Implement a schedule to collect customer feedback. It will help increase profits without a lot of cost and you are better able to get in front of a problem and maintain a good reputation. Once your reputation is ruined, it is very difficult and quite costly to get back.

GREAT CUSTOMER SERVICE BUILDS CREDIBILITY AND TRUST

As the population continues to age, joint replacements have become almost commonplace. Improved technology has meant that the new joints last longer and the surgeries to implant them are less risky. Yet in the late 2000's, some artificial hip joints manufactured by DePuy, a division of Johnson and Johnson, were found to be failing many years earlier than expected. This meant the patients who had them implanted had to have them removed and replaced.

Then a 2013 investigation revealed that DePuy had known that the hip joints were faulty a full year before they halted production and two years before they issued a recall. Countless patients went through the pain and expense of hip replacement surgery only to have a faulty joint implanted into their bodies. The fallout was horrendous: DePuy paid more than $4 billion dollars to settle over 7500 lawsuits.

Perhaps the worst thing a company can do is betray the trust of its customers. Most of the time such betrayal takes the form of knowingly selling a faulty service or product, as DePuy did, but sometimes betrayal simply comes in the form of promising something the company can't deliver. Consumers feel cheated when promotional materials offer multitudes of benefits that they ultimately fail to experience. For example, think of how you feel when a plumber or cable guy schedules a noon appointment and then shows up at 2:30, or when your local diner says "We're out of bacon." NO BACON? Would you ever trust that place again?

With whistleblowing stories like the DePuy fiasco flooding the headlines on a regular basis, consumers have become extra wary of trusting a company too soon. Providing great service gives your customers a good reason to have faith in what you're selling them. Serving your customers well communicates that you truly care about them, so they can trust you to act in their best interests.

Ironically, it was Tylenol, a different Johnson and Johnson subsidiary company, which set the standard for acting in its customers' best interests in 1982. The company was rocked by an unimaginable scandal when seven people died in the Chicago area after taking extra-strength Tylenol that had been laced with poison by a criminal. Even though the affected bottles were limited to the Chicago area, Tylenol immediately (and voluntarily) recalled all 31 million bottles of its product from stores, absorbing a loss of over 100 million dollars. It was one of the first safety related product recalls ever.

As Judith Rehak wrote in the New York Times decades later, "Marketers predicted that the Tylenol brand, which accounted for 17 percent of the company's net income in 1981, would never recover from the sabotage. But only two months later, Tylenol was headed back to the market, this time in tamper-proof packaging and bolstered by an extensive media campaign. A year later, its share of the $1.2 billion analgesic market, which had plunged to 7 percent from 37 percent following the poisoning, had climbed back to 30 percent."

People began buying Tylenol again because they trusted the company. Putting your customers first may initially cost a little more money, but the trust you gain is priceless.

REPEAT BUSINESS CHALLENGE

Take a moment in your next meeting to share a success story of building customer trust. Share trust-related feedback with your team to encourage action-oriented behavior. Trust with customers and employees is something that cannot be taken for granted, and must be reinforced on a daily basis. Like your reputation, once it is compromised, it is very difficult and time consuming to repair.

GREAT CUSTOMER SERVICE GIVES YOU A COMPETITIVE EDGE

Smart companies understand that customer service and marketing are not two entirely separate functions. They understand that their best possible advertisement is satisfied customers. This means that training your employees to provide consistently excellent customer service is not a luxury; it is just as vital to staying in business as making sure your website is properly maintained and your phone system works or most importantly that you have plenty of bacon.

Companies that treat customer service as a vital part of their marketing efforts also seek to provide value in every interaction with the consumer. This means that they are not constantly "selling," but rather focused on making sure that they are continually offering products, information or services that will actually make their customers' lives easier. Make sure your employees understand that if they are consistently taking care of their customers' needs, the sales will take care of themselves. As we'll discuss later in the book, connecting with your customers emotionally will do a lot more for generating repeat business than simply closing a sale in the short run.

Depending on your industry, you can drive traffic to your website by providing blog posts or articles that help solve your customers' problems. Search engine optimization (SEO) can help ensure that your company's blog shows up when people search for answers to questions related to your industry. Look for multiple ways to provide helpful, relevant content to your customers. Real estate agents might offer hints on fixing common household problems, while grocery stores can offer recipes and bacon-intensive meal solutions.

If you have a physical location, you can allow your customers to utilize it for community activities or needs. Some restaurants or stores allow community members to use a bulletin board to share local events, advertise for roommates or offer items for sale. Others may allow various groups to hold meetings or fundraisers at their facilities.

You can even create apps that help your customers with their problems, whether you possess the expertise in-house or you outsource that to a software specialist. Charmin toilet paper did this brilliantly when they created an app that allowed users to rate the cleanliness of public restrooms. Other users, particularly those with young children, could then access the information when traveling to know which restrooms to choose.

REPEAT BUSINESS CHALLENGE

Encourage every customer who had a positive experience to share their story on social media. Customer service is the new marketing. By making sure you are taking care of your customers' needs in a timely manner, with the right attitude and approach, your customers will become your biggest fans and your greatest source of advertisement.

RESOLVING A CUSTOMER SERVICE ISSUE SUCCESSFULLY WILL CREATE ADVOCATES FOR YOUR COMPANY

There is no foolproof way to create a perfect customer experience. The world is unpredictable, and depending on your industry there are multiple factors beyond your control that will have an impact on what happens when your customer is interacting with your business. Fortunately, a complaint is not the end of the world. In fact, according to Lee Resources, a customer who complains will do business with you again 70 percent of the time, as long as the complaint is resolved favorably.

Unfortunately, when such problems do occur, it is very easy to panic and try to avoid the customer altogether. Instead of trying to escape the situation, treat the customer's negative experience as an opportunity.

You may feel like receiving a customer complaint is just a bad thing that happens on a bad day, but in reality, the customer is giving you a chance to deepen your relationship with him or her in a positive way.

According to the White House Office of Consumer Affairs, for every customer who takes the trouble to bring you a complaint, 26 more stay silent. The customers who complain are not trying to ruin your day; they are offering you valuable insight into your market and how to best improve what you offer. As Kristin Smaby explains on her blog, *Being Human is Good Business,* "When customers share their story, they're not just sharing pain points. They're actually teaching you how to make your product, service, and business better. Your customer service organization should be designed to efficiently communicate those issues."

Make sure you not only take the time to respond to the customer, but that you also have a system in place to track complaints and ensure they are resolved favorably. Make it as easy as possible for customers to give feedback and be sure they know that you want the opportunity to make it right if they've had a bad experience. There are many ways to do this: comment cards, online forms, and so on. But most important is making sure your staff is properly trained to communicate—both verbally and non-verbally—that they truly want to make your customer's experience great and to correct it if it was less than great.

Once you and a customer have been through the experience of resolving a complaint, more often than not you will find that the two of you are more connected than you were before. This kind of experience can create a deeper impression on customers than if everything had gone perfectly, and will make them more likely to speak positively about your business to others. Remember, view complaints as an opportunity to deepen your relationship with your customers, and watch them become some of your strongest advocates.

REPEAT BUSINESS CHALLENGE

Discuss customer complaints and resolutions openly with your team. Train all employees to think about customer complaints in a positive, rather than negative way. Complaints are a way to learn, grow, and improve. As long as complaints are resolved quickly and not repeated, customers will continue to do business with you, and even recommend you. Communication is the key.

GREAT CUSTOMER SERVICE IMPROVES YOUR ONLINE RATINGS

We all know that the internet has forever changed the way consumers buy. According to information compiled by MineWhat, 81 percent of consumers will conduct online research before they purchase. Many marketing professionals emphasize these numbers when they're talking about the importance of an online presence and a user friendly website. However, the role the internet plays in keeping you in business goes far beyond the graphics you chose for your home page; it can bring you multitudes of new customers, or it can scare them away.

In addition to researching details and prices online, 61 percent of consumers will read an online customer product or service review before they make a decision, even if they are planning to purchase from a brick and mortar store. A Harvard Business School study found that a 1 star increase in Yelp ratings for restaurants led to a 5-9 percent increase in revenue. A study conducted by Cornell showed that positive online reviews for hotels allowed them to increase their prices without losing business.

The stronger your relationship with your customers, the happier they will be to go online and give you a positive review. Creating a positive online review doesn't cost the customer anything, but it does take effort. No matter how great your product or service is, if they felt you treated them with indifference, they are not likely to make the extra effort to give you a positive review. The more they feel you care about them, the more they will want to help your business out any way they can.

Of course online reviews are not all rainbows and unicorns. Every business will probably get a negative online review at some point in time. Even if you work to resolve every complaint to the customer's satisfaction, there will be some people who won't give you the opportunity to resolve it. Others may find pleasure in trashing any business online, particularly when they can remain anonymous. If you are providing excellent customer service, however, your positive reviews should overwhelm the negative ones.

When you see a negative review, try to send the customer a personal message and ask for the opportunity to make it right. Do NOT get defensive—no matter how obnoxious the customer is being— and do NOT confront the customer on Twitter or in any other public forum. Most people who post vitriolic online reviews are not sociopaths; they are usually venting their frustration at any number of things. If you reach out to them politely and graciously, most will be embarrassed by their own rude language and want to resolve the issue. As discussed in the previous section, many of these will become your staunchest advocates when it is all over.

Once a bad situation is resolved, encourage the customer to write honestly online about their experience. This lets others know that your company is committed to getting it right when things go wrong. If you have done all that can reasonably be done to address a customer complaint and the customer is still angry, it may be time to let it go and fire the customer. And reasonable people understand that some people are incurably unreasonable.

REPEAT BUSINESS CHALLENGE

Monitor online forums to see what your customers are saying about you and be sure to designate someone to respond to them. Implement a resolution strategy immediately to show the customer you are committed to resolving the issue. Respond publicly when warranted. It's also a good idea to monitor the comments of your competitors. The best way to ensure positive reviews is to exceed expectations at every level.

GREAT CUSTOMER SERVICE INCREASES YOUR COMPANY'S BOTTOM LINE

Staying in business is more challenging today than it has ever been. Your customer base could potentially span the globe, but so do your competitors. If you want to grow your market share and increase customer loyalty, you must commit to providing an unforgettable customer experience and resolving any problems that come up to the customer's satisfaction. In the face of global competition, you want to be the company that is keeping customers because they believe that you genuinely care about them.

Customer service is also one aspect of the market that you have complete control over. Only your company determines whether you give excellent customer service and work tirelessly to resolve every complaint. You may not always be able to undercut a competitor's price, but you can always do a better job serving the customer. It may be impossible for you to stay ahead of the curve with every technological advancement in your industry, but you can always train and retrain your people to have the best attitude, the most gracious manner and the most authentic smiles.

Imagine an army of hundreds, thousands or even millions of satisfied customers, buying from you over and over again, recommending your company to their friends and family, writing positive online reviews, and creating a positive impression of your company with new customers you haven't even met yet. That might sound far-fetched or idealistic, but that is exactly what you are building when you invest in excellent customer service. The benefits can't be measured just in quarterly earnings. The positive effect of great customer service on your bottom line will last for years and decades to come.

REPEAT BUSINESS CHALLENGE

Offer a referral incentive to people who are loyal customers. Excellent customer service is the best way to increase profits through referrals, recommendations and repeat business. Continuous training of employees is of the utmost importance if you want to turn customers into raving brand ambassadors.

SECTION II

WHAT YOUR CUSTOMERS WANT

Sometimes giving your customers what they want means letting them boo you off the stage.

Or something pretty close. As you might imagine, the circumstances that led to me being raucously booed in the line of duty were extreme to say the least. It was January, and a winter storm had dumped historic levels of snow on the East Coast, bringing several major cities—including Baltimore, Maryland and its harbor—to a complete standstill. The roads were altogether impassible, and residents were urged to venture out of their homes only in dire emergencies.

While the local children were doubtless thrilled to miss several days of school, the storm was a nightmare for countless businesses and their customers. For the cruise company I was a part of at the time, the situation literally called for all hands on deck. The ship I was on could not even get into our home port of Baltimore on the scheduled day, while the port workers themselves—baggage handlers, security personnel, inspectors and so on—were unable to leave their homes. This forced the company to extend a cruise by one day and shorten the next cruise by one day as well.

This was one of those decisions that was bound to make everyone unhappy, but there was no other feasible solution. Given the magnitude of the challenge, I was very proud to see all our departments work overtime to mitigate the unfortunate circumstances for our guests. On the ship itself, we immediately opened up the phone lines and internet café to allow guests to contact their loved ones for free. We did not charge extra fees or gratuities for the additional day, and we extended any benefits packages purchased by the guests for the extra day at no extra charge.

For those waiting for the next cruise in Baltimore, we quickly put notices on all of our websites, and we contacted all the travel agents we worked with to let them know the situation. Those who had booked their hotels through our company were not charged for the extra night, and all guests received an onboard credit—in proportion to the type of cabin they had booked—to compensate for the shortened cruise.

Unfortunately, once we finally got the guests for the second cruise aboard, there was more bad news to deliver. This was supposed to be a 10 day cruise to the Western Caribbean, but losing one day meant we could not make it to all the ports. Because of this, the company decided to do a 9 day cruise to the Eastern Caribbean, sending us to different islands than the guests were originally expecting. Before they got on the ship, the guests were offered the option of a full refund if they did not like the new itinerary. But since they had already made arrangements to be away, almost all chose to take the cruise anyway.

Although I knew I would have to bear the brunt of their displeasure, I realized I had to offer the guests the chance to express their feelings. So I brought up the change in itinerary at the initial meeting we had with the guests, and I let them boo me, so they could get their complaints out of their system. I understood that they wanted to be dealt with honestly, but they also wanted a chance to express their understandable disappointment and anger. Luckily for me, none of them had yet visited the buffet to stock up on tomatoes or eggs to throw.

Only after they were done expressing how they felt—and after they seemed convinced that I had heard them—did I crack a few jokes to lighten the mood. From that point on, everyone seemed to realize that each decision—however disappointing—had been made with their safety and security in mind. I assured them that we, as the crew, were also disappointed that we would not be able to give them the itinerary they had expected, and I promised they would still receive the same great service, food, entertainment and activities they would have otherwise.

By the end, both cruises (the one that was extended and the one that was shortened) received very high ratings from the guests in their satisfaction surveys. Despite extremely unusual and challenging circumstances that were completely out of our control, our staff had continued to focus on what we knew our customers wanted. And that ended up making all the difference.

PROACTIVE COMMUNICATION

Imagine two cable customers whose service goes out at 6:00 PM on a Friday. The first customer checks all his connections and can't figure out the problem. He calls the company and gets put on hold, because of course countless other customers are calling too. He grows more and more frustrated as he thinks about the friends that are coming over in an hour to watch a basketball game.

The second customer receives a text alert to her phone within minutes explaining that there is a service outage in her area, technicians are working on it, and she should expect her service to be restored within two hours. A subsequent text offers an apology for the inconvenience, thanks her for her loyalty and promises to inform her if anything changes.

These two customers are experiencing the identical challenge: an unexpected interruption in service. However the first customer is becoming increasingly angry, while the second feels only mildly inconvenienced. The only difference between the two is that the second person's company took the time to communicate proactively with its customers.

One of the greatest advantages of the digital age is it allows you to update your customers instantaneously about any changes, developments or problems with your business. Whether it's a change in your product or service, your prices, your hours of operation, method of delivery, your location or any number of other factors, there are now innumerable ways to inform your customers right away. The same goes for an unexpected challenge, like a breakdown in the computer system or a problem with one of your vendors or suppliers.

As we've already established, the world is not a perfect place. Your customers will be much more understanding with these inevitable imperfections if you proactively communicate with them about what is going wrong and what you are doing to fix it. Let your customers know what's happening, and when they can expect the problem to be resolved. Apologize for their inconvenience even though it isn't directly your fault. Just the fact that you care about their experience and take responsibility for it goes a long way toward helping most people overcome the personal inconvenience they may be experiencing.

You should also go out of your way to notify your customers of any new developments in your business, for example if your hours will change for a holiday. Nothing is more frustrating for loyal customers than to drive out of their way to visit your establishment only to realize that you are closed. It does not cost much to update your website and social media accounts on a regular basis to make sure your customers stay abreast of any deviations from your normal routine.

Ultimately, proactive communication with your customers lets them know you are always thinking about them. It allows you to frame any challenges that come up in the most favorable possible light, and it hopefully enables you to answer any questions your customers have before they ask. Proactive communication can even turn a problem into an opportunity to remind your customers how much you care.

REPEAT BUSINESS CHALLENGE

What is your proactive plan to address an issue? Review with your team possible ways to implement a communication system. Possible ways to address an issue:

- Send a text message or email to your customer letting them know you are aware of the issue and will address it immediately.
- Make a phone call addressing their concern and let them know you will update them as new information comes in to resolve their issue.

Proactive communication is vital to any business, especially when it concerns bad news. Make sure you have a plan in place before any such problem occurs, so that you can immediately jump into action to head off any negative reaction.

RESPECT

Many business leaders assume that training their employees to speak courteously is enough to make the customer feel respected. Yet the human need for respect goes far beyond just the desire to be treated politely. We all want to feel valued and taken seriously, especially when we are spending our hard earned money in a particular establishment when we could have gone somewhere else.

Small expressions of disrespect can have far reaching consequences for any relationship. Psychology professor John Gottman of the University of Washington has determined that eye-rolling after a spouse makes a comment is one of the strongest predictors of divorce. (Well, this and finishing the other person's curly fries without asking. Those are the two big no-nos) This tiny act—often committed unconsciously when the individual thinks no one is watching—betrays an inward disrespect of the person he or she should love the most.

It goes without saying that rolling one's eyes at a customer is completely unacceptable behavior, but there are countless other ways in which employees may unintentionally express similar disrespect. Failing to make eye contact, carrying on a personal conversation in the presence of a customer, checking a phone or being otherwise distracted are all ways in which an employee may communicate disrespect without realizing it. Particularly with younger workers, it may take intense and deliberate training to ensure your employees do not fall into any of these subtly disrespectful behaviors.

Of course respect goes both ways. The overwhelming majority of the time, you will find that going out of your way to demonstrate respect to your customers will prompt them to do the same for you. However, there are always the exceptions to this rule. At some point, you will undoubtedly encounter customers who go out of their way to be rude and disrespectful to you or your employees. The first thing to keep in mind in these situations is that your customers' behavior should not affect the standard at which you and your employees conduct yourselves. Again, even the most irate customers may calm down when they see your gracious response.

You must also make sure your employees are trained to deal with customers who may border on being out of control. Teach them to remain calm. It is important to maintain eye contact (if the interaction is in person) and a soft, steady tone of voice to demonstrate that you will not be intimidated or take an insult to heart. Your employees should know not to take the customer's rudeness personally, even if it is meant that way. Chances are, a rude customer would behave that way to anyone, so the bad attitude and even abusive words merely represent an opportunity for your employee to demonstrate their more mature response. Above all else, be certain your employees know that hurling a banana cream pie into the face of a shouting customer is never acceptable, no matter how fun, funny, and Twitter meme-inspiring it may be.

Employees must also know how to apologize sincerely to an obnoxious customer, without yielding to unreasonable demands. Be sure to give your employees a chance to decompress after being treated rudely or disrespectfully. If they don't have an opportunity to blow off steam about the situation, they may unintentionally carry the frustration over to the next customer. Take care to see they have someone to talk to about the interaction. (Naturally you must have appropriate security measures in place if a customer becomes an actual threat.)

At the end of the day, you must give respect to get respect, and teaching your employees respectful behavior is one of the best ways to win customers who will be loyal to you and your business.

REPEAT BUSINESS CHALLENGE

Host a workshop for your employees on how to handle frustration. While there may be a small upfront cost, the increase in your bottom line due to satisfied customers will be a reward many times over. Respect is a basic human need; in everyday life and in business. It is vital that all employees realize the importance of respect for customers, fellow workers, and most importantly, for themselves.

TO HAVE THEIR PROBLEMS TAKEN SERIOUSLY

Imagine taking your daughter to the hospital. She is burning up with a fever and has a strange rash all over her body. You are understandably distressed, but you are trying to stay calm for her sake. When you finally see the doctor, he greets you and examines your daughter casually. He checks his phone, ducks out for a chat with a nurse, and then assures you that your daughter has a virus that has been going around, and it's nothing to worry about. He tells you to go home, put her to bed, and give her lots of fluids.

Even if the doctor's diagnosis was one hundred percent correct, you would probably be pretty upset with how he treated you. Why? Because even if that doctor had seen 200 patients that month with exactly the same illness, the fact that your daughter was sick that night was still a big deal to you.

When you work in a particular industry, whether it is retail, healthcare, academia or hospitality, you become an expert in that field. You quickly develop your own vocabulary and become familiar with all the little things that can go wrong. But for most of your customers, your industry is something of a mystery. Something that is "no big deal" to you may still be very disturbing to them.

Depending on what you do, your customers may only come in contact with your company on a special occasion. A server in a restaurant serves hundreds of plates of food each week. But the family he is serving at table 16 may only go out to eat once in a while. They may be celebrating a birthday or another big milestone, and they understandably want it to be perfect. If anything goes wrong you want to make sure you take into account that the issue may be marring their special time.

Now sometimes it can be reassuring to a customer to know that a particular problem is fairly common or nothing to worry about. For example, turbulence on an airplane or rough waters on a ship may cause passengers discomfort, but such commonplace occurrences can also cause them anxiety if they think that they are in danger. But even if your intention is to assure the passengers that the problem is not a threat, you want to take care that you are not unintentionally communicating to them that you are indifferent to their comfort or how well their vacation is going.

Taking your customers' problems seriously is vital to staying in business in a competitive economy. It shows them respect and demonstrates that you care about the experience they are having with your company. Make sure your employees understand this, and that they also know how to educate customers respectfully about the problem when it is helpful.

Even if what goes wrong is relatively minor—or even the result of a customer mistake rather than a mistake that you or one of your employees made—take the complaint seriously. See it as an opportunity to demonstrate how much you really do value that particular customer. Whenever possible, go above and beyond to ensure their experience with your company is everything they hoped for and more.

REPEAT BUSINESS CHALLENGE

Roleplay with your team members' potential situations that could cause your customer distress and implement effective communication techniques to minimize and manage their concerns. The quickest way to drive your customers into the open arms of your competitors is to not take them or their problems seriously. Always go one step above what is expected to create a personal, long lasting relationship.

TO BE SERVED PROMPTLY

We all know that everyone is in a hurry these days. Almost all of us are juggling a career, a family and various other pursuits. That means that our time is a precious commodity, whether it's our time on the phone or in an establishment. Our time is still valuable whether it is spent on your company's website or sending you an email. So if your website is difficult to navigate or you don't respond to an email promptly, you are communicating that you do not value your customers' time. Even if you offer the best product or service value for the price you charge, customers will flock to your competition if you waste their time.

You want your customers' interactions with you to be efficient and smooth. Furthermore, any time your customers spend interacting with your business but not being served effectively is also wasting your company's time and resources. Efficiency benefits everyone concerned, as long as you don't sacrifice the human touch in the process.

If there must be a wait—and sometimes there must—do all you can to make it pleasant. If you have a wait at your call center, there are now automated services that allow your employees to call a customer back when they become available, rather than forcing the customer to wait on the phone. Some restaurants serve complementary appetizers when the wait for a table is unusually long. Doctors' and dentists' offices offer video games and plenty of entertainment for young children. (Some doctors and dentists even have a soundproof separate room for children, with free appetizers and Happy Hour drinks for the parents. What? They don't? Well, they should.) Retail and food service employees should be empowered to offer coupons or other rewards for customers who have had to wait an unusually long time. All of these amenities help you stay in business, because they make customers want to patronize your business over a competitor's.

It goes without saying that your physical establishment should have a comfortable, clean waiting room for customers. Train your employees to apologize for a wait time that is above what should be expected in your industry, and you should be willing to cover any extra cost to rush shipping on an order that should have been ready earlier.

Lastly, take your commitments to contact a customer back very seriously. This goes to the heart of your integrity as a business. Nothing is more frustrating than to be promised an email or a call by a particular time and not to receive it. And if your customers cannot trust you to keep your word in such a simple matter, they will have difficulty trusting anything else you say.

Even if you do not have an answer or a solution for customers by the time you have promised to contact them, reach out and let them know you are still working on it. This is essential to building trust, and it lets them know you care about them and are doing your best to serve them well.

REPEAT BUSINESS CHALLENGE

Ask customers directly how they feel about your company's ability to manage time. Is there something they would like if avoiding a wait is impossible? Implement a suggestion and gather feedback. In today's hectic, rushed environment, time is of the essence. Taking the time of your customers for granted, making them wait long periods for any type of service, whether it's a first time visitor, or someone dealing with a problem, will make them think twice about doing business with you again.

TO BE LISTENED TO

One of the most fundamental and profound ways to demonstrate respect is to give someone your full attention. Purposeful, empathetic listening is particularly challenging for younger workers who may not have much practice. Make sure your employees are trained to maintain eye contact, nod to show they understand and ask questions when appropriate. They should also know not to fidget or otherwise communicate through their body language that they are trying to speed the conversation along.

Employees should also be trained to be self-aware so that they do not interrupt. Interrupting—even when it is meant well—can come across as particularly disrespectful. Some people talk faster than others and may unintentionally interrupt a slower speaker. Whatever your intention, interrupting says that you believe what you have to say is more important than what the other person is saying.

There are several obstacles to attentive listening that you may face when interacting with customers. First, if the customer is making a complaint, you may find yourself feeling defensive. Remember not to take the complaint personally, but rather (as we've already emphasized) look at it as an opportunity to help you and the company improve. Second, some customers may be very long winded, taking many words to explain something that could be said much more concisely. In these cases, it can be very tempting to become impatient as you wait for the customer to finish his or her point; this is especially true if you are very busy and have a long list of tasks to complete. Remind yourself to show the customer the same respect you would want in his or her situation; try picturing your parent or grandparent in the customer's place (No, not that grandparent, the other one. Not the one who gave you sweaters for your birthday, the one who gave you money and a puppy and let you drink wine at Thanksgiving when you were a teenager.), and listen the way you would want someone to listen to them.

Third, some customers will make a statement that is untrue or erroneous while they are speaking to you, and it can be very tempting to try to jump in and correct them. The old maxim "The customer is always right," only goes so far. In reality, there may be many times that the customer is flat out wrong about something, but there is a correct time and way to offer accurate information. Almost always, an indirect correction will work best.

Fourth, some customers may be upset for a reason that is totally unrelated to their interaction with your company. They may be frustrated for any number of reasons and are simply taking it out on you or your employees, or trying to extend the conversation in order to seek a sympathetic ear. Train your employees to recognize these situations and respond with kindness and understanding. On the other hand a customer may be excited about something unrelated to your company—a new grandchild or a promotion at work—may simply be eager to share their good news with someone. Remember that part of building a relationship with your customers is listening to these personal anecdotes, even when you are busy.

Bartenders understand that listening to stories of woe or excitement is part of their job. In reality, the same can be true at times of anyone who interacts directly with customers.

REPEAT BUSINESS CHALLENGE

Conduct an exercise with your team focused on listening. Often people are unaware of how often they interrupt so this would be a good opportunity to respectfully bring it to their attention. This cannot be stressed often enough: listening is the key to all successful communication, in life and in business. Train your employees in the art of listening, and explain how it will enhance their personal and professional development. And then reinforce that training again and again.

PROMPT ATTENTION TO A COMPLAINT OR CONCERN

Open communication is the key to serving your customers, especially when they bring a complaint or a concern to your attention. If the problem is something you are able to address immediately, then do so. But if the issue is more complicated, be sure to update them on your progress.

As we've already discussed, the problem with keeping your customers waiting is not just that it makes them feel impatient. It is frustrating to the customer not to know what is going on. Whether it is food taking too long at a restaurant, an appliance that is taking too long to be delivered or a car that is taking too long to be repaired, your customers want to be kept up to date on the situation. And of course even if the delay is caused by something out of your control, let them know, but still apologize sincerely for the inconvenience it is causing them.

To stay in business, you want to be sure that you have well understood protocols in place for the appropriate time frame for a company response to a complaint. When the nature of the problem is not particularly time sensitive, a good rule of thumb may be to respond to phone calls within 24 hours and emails within 48 hours. Remember, make contact even if you don't have a resolution for them yet. Just let them know where you are in the process and what is going on. This will help the customer know that you do care about their problem and you are working to resolve it as quickly as you can.

Depending on your industry, you may need to have someone available to serve customers after normal business hours. You may want to hire someone specifically to deal with this, or you may want to distribute the responsibility to a large number of your employees based on a rotating schedule. This way, no one employee has to be "on duty" on the weekends and evenings all the time.

It's impossible to stay in business if your customers feel ignored or neglected when they bring you complaints and concerns. Find a method and a system that works for your company and make sure that your employees are properly trained to carry it out. Otherwise, you risk pushing your customers to your competition.

REPEAT BUSINESS CHALLENGE

Have an honest discussion about your response time to customers. Ask your team what steps can be taken to close the gap on how quickly you can respond. To increase repeat business, always respond quickly and appropriately to a problem or concern. Statistics overwhelmingly show customers will do business with you again, and recommend you to others, if you are able to resolve problems and concerns in a timely manner.

RESTITUTION FOR TIME AND EFFORT

"Sorry, ma'am," the customer service representative said regretfully, "We are not allowed to give you the upgrade to stainless steel." Laura had been on the phone with the home warranty company countless times over the past several months trying to get her dishwasher replaced. The company had repaired the appliance twice and finally agreed to replace it when it broke a third time. Unfortunately, because the company's contractors had taken several weeks with each unsuccessful repair, Laura had been without a dishwasher for over 100 days. Now the company was informing her they would not pay for a stainless steel upgrade so that the new one would match her other appliances.

Remember that to make something "right" with a customer who has had a negative experience, you must go beyond just refunding any money they have spent on a product or a service that did not meet their expectations. If they spent time and energy getting the problem addressed, they want to know that their inconvenience matters to you. Making it right includes restitution for their difficulties.

Technically, Laura's home warranty company had done nothing wrong. Their representatives were polite and apologized to her for her inconvenience. They fulfilled their obligation by replacing her appliance, and according to her contract, they were not obligated to replace it with the same color. But they failed to recognize that their contractors' inability to complete the repairs and subsequent replacement in a timely manner cost Laura countless hours washing dishes by hand as well as on the phone trying to get the problem fixed. She experienced their unwillingness to upgrade the appliance as more than just a refusal to make an exception to their rigid policies. To her, it was an insult and a statement that her incredible inconvenience didn't matter to the company. She immediately began researching competitors and asking friends and relatives for recommendations.

To stay in business, you must keep your customers happy. Remember how much less it costs to keep an existing customer compared to the cost of landing a new one. According to Laura's calculations, the 74 dollar expense to upgrade her appliance would have worked out to less than 25 cents for each hour she spent washing dishes by hand. This relatively small amount of money would have been a sign, however, that the company took her inconvenience seriously. Don't treat your customers like their time and energy do not matter, especially when something has gone wrong. Show them that you care, even if it costs you a little more.

REPEAT BUSINESS CHALLENGE

Implement a policy to personally connect with customers about how you appreciate the valuable time they took to express their concerns. While it may cost you a little more in the short term, going above and beyond what is expected to fix a problem will create lasting dividends in the long term.

TO FEEL VALUED MORE THAN THE NEW CUSTOMERS YOU ARE PURSUING

Imagine you and four friends have been working with a nonprofit organization to restore a community center. Every Saturday for six months you throw out trash, clean bathrooms, wash windows, scrub floors and repaint walls. On the morning the center is going to reopen, 20 new volunteers show up to help the five of you decorate for the occasion. They spend an hour blowing up balloons and hanging banners, and everything looks great.

At the big ceremony, the leader of the nonprofit invites all 25 volunteers up together and thanks all of you for helping make the day possible. She makes no distinction between the five of you who labored for six long months doing very unpleasant tasks and the 20 who showed up an hour before it opened. How would you feel?

Even if you donated your time and effort out of completely generous motivations, you would likely feel at least a little annoyed that your contribution was not being distinguished from that of the people who donated just an hour of their time. But now imagine that the leader hadn't recognized you at all. Imagine that she had called the twenty new volunteers up, showered them with praise for their decoration services, and offered them $100 gift cards as a token of her appreciation. All the while, you and your four friends were standing in the audience, completely ignored.

That is exactly how loyal customers feel when a company showers gifts and other promotional offers to try to win over new customers. This is especially true if they offer newer customers lower rates on a service or lower prices on a product than those customers that have been with them for years. Your customers want to feel that they are at least as important to you as the new customers you are pursuing through your marketing efforts.

All these issues will be greatly reduced, if not entirely eliminated, if you develop strong, authentic relationships with your customers.

REPEAT BUSINESS CHALLENGE

Develop a quarterly strategy to touch base with customers and thank them for their business. Don't forget how important your existing customers are to the growth of your business. Special deals and incentives will keep them coming back long after new customers leave for the next short term opportunity. Develop a tiered approached to keep your most loyal customers coming back, and they will bring more new customers with them.

GOOD VALUE

If you take the time to read negative reviews of almost any business—whether it is a retail store, a restaurant, or a vacation resort—the most common indictment of a bad experience is that the unsatisfied customers felt like they wasted their money. A bad purchasing decision can leave anyone feeling disappointed, frustrated, or even angry. And when we feel that way, we usually do more than just resolve not to repeat the mistake. We often make it our mission to warn others away from the business in question.

Offering good value has everything to do with meeting or exceeding your customers' expectations. If you bought a $5 rain poncho at an amusement park and it lasted a year, you would probably be pretty pleased. On the other hand, if you bought a $100 rain jacket and it lasted two years, you would probably feel fairly upset. The second item lasted longer, but it was a much worse value for what you paid.

Whatever your price point or target market, everyone wants to feel like they are receiving good value for their money. Whether a restaurant sells a ten dollar meal or a one hundred dollar meal, customers want to feel like they got what they paid for, or even a little more. Receiving good value makes us feel more than just satisfied; it makes us want to tell others so they can benefit too.

To stay in business, make sure your customers feel like they are getting good value, whatever your industry and whatever your target market. Remember to look for ways to bring additional value to your customers' experience with you. Create content or services that will make them feel like they are being helped, educated and served when they are interacting with your business.

REPEAT BUSINESS CHALLENGE

Review your competitor's product and their customer experience as compared to your own. What can you implement to show more value? Studies and surveys have repeatedly shown that consumers will spend more if they know they will receive a superior product or service. No matter how much they spend, your customers want to know they are getting a good, if not great, return on their investment of time and money. Continually monitor the price points of your products and services to make sure they are in line with expectations. How do you know? Ask!

AN HONEST DEAL

In 2015, AT&T was forced by the FCC to pay $100 million dollars in fines for misleading its customers about their "unlimited data plans." According to CNN, "AT&T subjected its unlimited data plan customers to significantly slower speeds after they used more than 3 GB of 3G data or 5 GB of 4G data in a single billing cycle. AT&T then failed to adequately notify its customers that their speeds would be throttled after they crossed a certain data threshold, the FCC said."

Other cell phone companies have been known to place bogus charges on their customers' bills, counting on the fact that most of them are too busy to carefully look through every item. But plenty of other industries are also known for intentionally cheating their customers. We've all met a few salesmen who will say anything to close a deal, and auto mechanics or contractors who will mislead you about what is really wrong with your car or your house. Although such individuals may get money from a customer in the short term, they will pay in the long term with poor reputations, lack of referrals and poor customer reviews. "Penny wise and Pound foolish" isn't just a saying, it's the truth. (So is "Never argue with a cop" but that's not relevant here.)

Many companies also claim to offer better deals by disguising the real price of their product or service. The advertised price is often just a "base" with additional fees added on to make the purchase actually work as promised. Others offer low introductory rates and gradually raise the price without announcing it. The short term result of all these tactics is that the customer feels cheated. And customers who feel cheated will always be looking for better options.

To stay in business, your customers must feel like they are getting an honest deal. If they don't, online reviews, social media and other consumer advisory services will soon let the world know. But beyond your reputation, you must also guard your integrity. At the end of the day, we all want to feel proud of what we do and so do our employees. When you give your customers an honest deal, you can.

REPEAT BUSINESS CHALLENGE

Discuss with your team how you're marketing your products and services. Are you transparent with your customers? Nothing is more important than the trust you establish with your customers. It can take a long time to build that relationship, but once it is broken, it may never be restored. If something happens to question that trust, be open, honest, and accountable. Make it right immediately to lessen any potential long-term damage.

REWARDS FOR LOYALTY

No one likes to be taken for granted in any relationship. When we are there for others—steadily and faithfully—over long periods of time, we like to be periodically reminded that our efforts are not going unnoticed. While this sentiment is strongest among family members and friends, it extends to business relationships as well.

Your loyal customers—the ones who buy from you over and over again—want to be appreciated. Take the time to thank them on a regular business for patronizing your business. If you don't already, put a loyalty program in place to reward your customers that buy from you most frequently or in the largest quantity. Of course offering perks to new customers may be an important part of your marketing efforts, but don't allow those perks to overshadow the benefits your loyal customers get.

There are several different kinds of loyalty programs that reward your best customers in meaningful ways but don't break the bank for you. You can implement a points system that rewards the number of purchases or the dollar value of each purchase, offering benefits or perks at certain benchmarks. This has the advantage of helping your customers feel that they are earning while they buy. Another option is to charge an upfront fee for preferred customer benefits, like Amazon Prime or Costco membership. This makes customers feel like they are investing in their patronage of your company, so they will be more inclined to purchase from you in order to get the most out of their investment.

Other types of loyalty programs include partnering with other companies to offer benefits or developing customized profiles to make the purchasing process faster and simpler. Remember, a good loyalty program should not take a lot of time for your customers to manage or accrue benefits. Most people do not have the patience to keep track of punch cards or coupons (electronic accounts will avoid those hassles); they simply want to benefit from purchasing from you, rather than from your competitors.

REPEAT BUSINESS CHALLENGE

It is important to have some sort of Loyalty Program in place to thank your long time customers, as mentioned above. Discuss directly with your customers what they would like to see as a reward for being loyal. They will bring great ideas to the table. To really make them feel special, a hand written *Thank You* note goes a long way to fostering a personal relationship that has developed over time. It costs little, but creates a lasting memory.

CONSISTENCY

Consistency is extremely important in any relationship. We expect our friends and family members to treat us with love and respect no matter what is going on. Similarly, we expect the companies we patronize to offer us consistent quality and service whenever we buy from them. In fact, a study conducted by McKinsey and Company of nearly 30,000 Americans found that "a consistent customer experience across the entire customer journey will increase customer satisfaction, build trust and boost loyalty."

Remember customer satisfaction is closely related to meeting or exceeding the customers' expectations regarding price, quality and service. Think about how comforting it is to be able to get the same cup of coffee whether you are in a strange town, an airport or around the corner from your house. Most of us are even willing to pay a little extra to know that we are getting what we expect.

Consistency is vital to staying in business in a competitive market. But how do we deliver a consistent customer experience?

Writing in *Forbes*, Micah Solomon explains what it takes: "[You] need to be able to deliver customer service precisely as you wish it to be delivered—over and over and over. This requires knowing how to design, introduce, and reinforce customer service standards."

In short, to deliver a consistent customer experience, you need clear standards, a clear communication of those standards to your employees, and clear reinforcement of those standards on a regular basis. You will also need to recruit and hire employees who will be able to deliver at the standards you require. In the next section, we'll cover how to do exactly that.

REPEAT BUSINESS CHALLENGE

Discuss your standards with your team and put in place a system to ensure they are being met. Consistency with your product or service is imperative to keeping loyal, repeat customers. Make sure your employees are trained on a regular basis to keep a positive attitude in delivering consistency. They must realize the benefits to them as employees, as well as to the long term viability of the business.

SECTION III

WHAT YOUR EMPLOYEES NEED TO PROVIDE MORE THAN PERFECT CUSTOMER SERVICE

I think I'm going to turn in my two weeks' notice," the young man said to me sadly.

I was shocked. Victor had just started as a sports staff member, and we all had high hopes for him. For many, being part of the sports staff is a dream job; you might be helping cruise guests with a zip line harness one moment and organizing a volleyball tournament the next. Victor had been hired for his great energy, terrific attitude and of course his infectious love of sports. So why was he ready to throw in the towel so soon?

As the division head, I called Victor into my office for a heart to heart chat. In response to my questions, he explained that he had been receiving some negative comments from guests. He also expressed his uncertainty about his duties and how he just didn't feel at ease on the ship. After listening to him for a few minutes the problem was clear; he had never been properly trained to give the service he wanted to give.

A little investigating on my part soon confirmed that the supervisor who had trained Victor was leaving our company soon, and had not put much effort into showing him the ropes. Victor had essentially been thrown into the deep end of the pool and told to figure out how to swim. No wonder he was frustrated and ready to leave!

I asked Victor to stay for two more weeks, work with a new supervisor and give the job another chance. I told him I would personally get involved to make sure he was receiving the proper instruction, as well as a clear understanding of all policies and procedures that he should have had all along. He cautiously agreed.

As soon as he began working with a new supervisor, Victor's entire demeanor was transformed. He began to thrive in his new position and quickly became one of our highest rated sports staff members. Clearly on the path to becoming a supervisor himself, he told me he will definitely make sure all new hires in his care will receive everything they need to provide more than perfect service to his customers.

Now that we have covered why superior customer service is vital to staying in business and what your customers want from you, it's time to discuss in more detail what your employees need to deliver this kind of service. All of us have our own unique personalities, but we are also influenced by the people around us. For example, people who are normally very quiet may go to a football game and scream until they lose their voices, because they get caught up in the atmosphere of the game. The same is true of a boisterous person who attends a memorial service. He will likely respond to the solemnity of the occasion by behaving differently than he normally would. In short, we each respond to the environment we are in by adjusting our behavior.

Whether we realize it or not, we do this in our workplace environment as well. In fact, because we spend such a large percentage of our time there, the atmosphere in a company can end up having a profound effect on everyone who works there. Ultimately, it can bring out the best or the worst in us. The good news is that when you create a workplace culture where excellent customer service is the norm, it actually becomes easier and more natural for all your employees to give that service.

To create this kind of environment, you must set clear expectations from the very beginning. You must also make sure your employees have the knowledge and skills outlined in this section. You can do this by providing initial and ongoing training opportunities to ensure they can learn, grow and improve. You also want to be sure that you explain your company culture during the interview process with any potential employees so you can be sure to hire individuals who share your values and will fit in well.

While the list in this section is not exhaustive, you can be confident that if your employees are able to master these items, you will consistently give your customers more than perfect service.

COMMUNICATION SKILLS

Communication skills are absolutely vital to providing more than perfect customer service. While communication is very simply the transfer of information from one person to another, to do so clearly and respectfully is not always an easy task. Depending on the situation, you may also want your employees to be able to demonstrate warmth, kindness, compassion or even excitement when they communicate. These skills come naturally to some, but others need to be methodically trained and given opportunities to practice.

Perhaps the most important communication skill is listening. What? Listening. What, now? LISTENING! We have already covered the importance of offering your customers a listening ear, but how can you ensure that your employees have the needed skills to do this consistently? In reality, most of us are not natural listeners, so we need to be deliberately taught how to listen effectively, especially in a customer service context. This can be particularly challenging when your employees face pressure to handle a large volume of calls or in-person customer interactions.

Start training your employees in effective listening skills as part of their new hire orientation. This is part of protecting your culture and ensuring new employees don't develop any bad habits. They should understand how to smile and make eye contact to show the customer that they care and are paying attention. Make sure that they know not to jump to conclusions about what a customer is trying to say, but rather listen carefully until the customer is finished talking. Depending on your industry, it may be important to teach them to take notes on what a customer is saying in order to keep track of any important details.

Good communicators enunciate clearly, use careful diction and concise speech. There is nothing wrong with having an extended conversation with a customer in the right context, but you do not want your employees to take 30 words to communicate information that could be conveyed effectively in ten. Teach your employees to be aware of and to control their own non-verbal communication—facial expressions, body language, tone of voice—as well as monitor these cues in those they are speaking to. This is especially important if the customer is flustered or having trouble getting to the point.

Ultimately, you want your employees to be able to communicate with both confidence and humility. They should know how to leave customers with the assurance that they have been heard and taken seriously. The best part is that these skills are not only beneficial at work; they can help employees improve their personal relationships as well.

REPEAT BUSINESS CHALLENGE

Set up a communication workshop for your employees and encourage open door policies to express needs and concerns. Communication skills are so important; you cannot leave them to chance. Make sure all front of house employees have been properly trained in excellent communication skills. This can be done in a classroom setting or online. Toastmasters International is a worldwide organization helping individuals improve their communication, public speaking and leadership skills. Look for a club in your area.

EMPATHY

No one's honeymoon is perfect, but when stormy weather canceled every flight in and out of Tampa, FL Dave and Marcia thought they were going to have to miss their cruise and spend their first days of wedded bliss in the Atlanta airport! Their initial pleas for help to the disinterested woman behind the counter of "Airline X" were dismissed. With an impatient sigh, she assured them that it was simply impossible to get them to Tampa in time to meet their cruise ship.

A more humane individual behind the counter of "Airline Y" overheard their story and offered to help. Within minutes she had booked them on a flight to Orlando and arranged for a limousine service (which the couple was happy to pay for) to drive them the 90 minutes to Tampa in time to meet their cruise ship. With a few clicks of a mouse, the Airline Y employee was able to make the "impossible" happen for Dave and Marcia. This was not because she was necessarily more talented than the Airline X employee, but because her imagination and problem solving skills were activated by her authentic care for the couple in distress.

Nothing is more powerful in a customer service interaction than an employee who genuinely empathizes with a customer and his or her situation. We all have an inner gauge for how concerned another person is for our situation, and if we sense that someone genuinely cares, it moves us. When we experience genuine empathy, we are grateful.

People who are truly empathetic actually feel the emotion the other person is feeling, even if they do not experience it quite as strongly. Contrary to popular belief, empathy is not something we are necessarily endowed with at birth. We can learn to be empathetic and we can practice expressing it. We can all take the time to imagine ourselves in someone else's shoes, and allow ourselves to share what that person is going through.

Remember that empathy really depends on your willingness to listen carefully and express it, not on how easily the person you are dealing with actually evokes empathy. In fact, hostage negotiators are trained to communicate empathetically with terrorists, many of whom are undoubtedly difficult to sympathize with. Writing in *Psychology Today*, David F. Swink explains,

> *"Hostage negotiators are trained to act empathetically toward the hostage taker in order to establish the rapport necessary to influence him to give up and not hurt anyone. In fact, the negotiator most likely despises a person that would hold a woman and baby as hostages. What is interesting is that after a couple of hours many negotiators actually start to feel some empathy toward the hostage taker as a result of 'acting' empathetic."*

Of course empathy starts at the top. Daniel Goleman, author of *Emotional Intelligence,* remarks, "Leaders with empathy do more than sympathize with people around them: they use their knowledge to improve their companies in subtle, but important ways." He goes on to explain that they "thoughtfully consider employees' feelings – along with other factors – in the process of making intelligent decisions." We'll cover much more about what you need to lead an organization this way in section four.

REPEAT BUSINESS CHALLENGE

Develop an exercise with employees where the objective is to "get in the mind" of the customer. It's a fun exercise that is also critical in developing strategies to better help customers. Empathy is hard to teach; it really is more of an attitude of wanting to help people. Having the right attitude is the basic foundation for More Than Perfect® service. Remember to "Hire for Attitude, train for skill".

WHAT YOUR EMPLOYEES NEED TO PROVIDE
MORE THAN PERFECT CUSTOMER SERVICE

AN EYE FOR SAFETY AND SECURITY

You want your business to be a safe place for your employees and your customers. This may involve something as simple as ensuring the sidewalks in front of your building are properly shoveled after a winter snow storm. It could also require something as complicated as commissioning a special software program to ensure that all your customers' personal information is protected when they interact with your website.

Not all of us are born with a natural eye for safety, but when you have a new baby, you immediately become attuned to anything that could threaten that baby's wellbeing. (Which every new parent discovers are EVERYWHERE.) You are suddenly alert to anyone with a cold or mild illness who could unintentionally infect your child. You carry hand sanitizer with you everywhere and ensure that all the baby's toys are kept clean. As he or she learns to crawl, you notice choking hazards everywhere, as well as flights of stairs, sharp edges, (polar bears wandering into your Arizona desert home, meteors - you know, realistic threats) and so on.

You want your employees to begin to develop a "parent's eye" for the safety of your customers and your business. Point out potential dangers to everyone when you notice them, so that they can begin to notice things on their own. You might even want to offer a small incentive or reward for employees that bring a potential safety or security threat to your attention.

If you have any doubts about how to identify hazards around your business, the United States Department of Labor Occupational Safety and Health Administration (OSHA) has many resources to help. This includes an interactive hazard identification tool that is designed both to teach business owners and their workers "the process for finding hazards in their workplace," and to "raise awareness on the types of information and resources about workplace hazards available on OSHA's website."

You also want to make sure that your employees are fully trained for emergencies. Depending on your industry, it might make sense to offer a CPR certification course to your staff and to have a first aid kit handy. If there is any particular kind of emergency you are likely to encounter, you probably want to have regular drills so you are certain everyone knows what to do.

Of course not all threats are physical in nature. Customers can face threats to their property, and data breaches can jeopardize their personal information. Although many consumer advocates complain that data breaches don't cause significant negative consequences for the companies that allow them, retail giant Target saw their quarterly profits drop substantially as a result of a 2013 breach.

According to the New York Times, "The widespread theft of Target customer data had a significant impact on the company's profit, which fell more than 40 percent in the fourth quarter [of 2013]..." Of course those losses came in addition to the 39 million dollar class action settlement with the banks and the 40 million customers who were significantly inconvenienced by the breach.

Most workplace hazards will not rise to that level, but teaching your employees to have an eye for safety is the first step to eliminating dangers, large and small.

REPEAT BUSINESS CHALLENGE

Safety and Security for customers and employees needs to be a top priority, and it starts with awareness. Have monthly meetings that address all types of safety and security issues, which can include the physical building where you work, as well as all personal information. Bring in experts if needed.

WHAT YOUR EMPLOYEES NEED TO PROVIDE
MORE THAN PERFECT CUSTOMER SERVICE

AN EYE FOR FIRST IMPRESSIONS AND ATTENTION TO DETAIL

A lipstick mark on a glass or a dull steak knife can cast a cloud over an otherwise perfect dining experience. On the other hand, a perfect bottle of wine or a beautifully crafted dessert can make a great experience unforgettable. Even when we first gaze at a masterpiece of art or architecture, it is often the cumulative impact of the tiniest details that fills us with awe.

To offer the best possible experience for your customers, you and your employees must cultivate an eye for first impressions and attention to detail. This includes the details of the cleanliness and presentation of their own personal appearance and of the physical location of your business. It also holds true for the details of written communication, the company's online presence and social media accounts and any advertising or promotional materials.

Remember that the details of your foyer, atrium and even your website and Facebook page create the first impression customers will ever have of your business. Just like first impressions are vital to selling a home or a car, and a first date can make or break a relationship, the feelings your customers have when they encounter your business for the first time have a very long lasting effect. If they are positive, it will be that much easier to engage them and win them over. If those feelings are negative, you have an uphill climb ahead.

Psychologists and neurologists alike agree that first impressions are far more powerful than they ought to be from a purely rational point of view. Sometimes called the "Halo Effect"—a term coined by psychologist Edward Thorndike in a 1920 paper—positive overall impressions cause us to make all sorts of subsequent assumptions in favor of the person, organization or object in question. In the same way we may subconsciously assume that an attractive woman is kind or that a tall man is a good leader, we assume that a business with a neat, professional appearance will offer the best quality goods or services.

Training is essential. Not everyone is naturally detail oriented, so be sure all your employees know what they need to pay attention to. You do not want to create an environment where your employees feel criticized all the time, or where an employee who is generally satisfactory feels discouraged over a relatively minor mistake or oversight. Instead, you want to generate excitement over getting things "more than perfect" for your guests. To do this be sure to compliment employees when things look the way they are supposed to, as well as pointing out when something is out of place.

REPEAT BUSINESS CHALLENGE

The best way to find out about first impressions and attention to detail is to ask! Ask your customers, but also ask your employees. Have your employees, especially new hires, walk in the shoes of the customer. Have them experience the same conditions your customers go through, from going on your website to walking in your front door. Have them fill out questionnaires or surveys. If you feel you will get more honest results, have them do it anonymously.

THE AUTHORITY TO SOLVE PROBLEMS

By the time a customer says, "I want to speak to a manager," something has probably gone very, very wrong. Those words indicate that the customer has remained unsatisfied or become frustrated and certainly has not been able to resolve his or her problem with the employee initially in charge of handling the issue. And by the time a complaint has been brought to a manager, the employee is probably pretty frustrated as well.

But of course for many businesses, this is exactly how the process is supposed to work. Many companies structure their response protocol for customer complaints in a way that makes it extremely difficult for customers to actually get their problem resolved. The idea is that if you put enough obstacles in their way, eventually customers will just give up. This is true enough. People are busy, and eventually they will get tired of trying to get their problem resolved. But it also means that they will happily leave you for a competitor at the earliest opportunity.

It should go without saying that this is no way to provide more than perfect service. Not only does it frustrate your customers, it is terrible for employee morale. One of the reasons that many employees are reluctant to engage with a customer who has a problem is that they feel like there is nothing they can do to help the person. Offering a listening ear and a polite, caring response is incredibly important, but it will only go so far if the employee is not empowered to actually solve the customer's problem.

Of course there are unreasonably demanding customers or unusually challenging problems, but these tend to make up a very small percentage of the complaints your employees will need to field. Develop an array of solutions that you are comfortable allowing your front-line customer service representatives to utilize when they judge it to be appropriate. Then give them the freedom to offer those solutions without coming to management every single time.

Almost all employees are happy to engage a customer with a problem when they feel empowered and trained to solve it. Empowered employees save the company time by preventing the vast majority of customer complaints from escalating to the level of requiring manager input. They also greatly reduce the customer's frustration by resolving the issue quickly. On the other hand, disempowered employees are essentially being used as shields to absorb the customers' complaints, while protecting management from having to deal with them. This model does not cultivate loyal customers, and it inevitably leads to costly employee turnover. And you don't have to be a management genius to know that's no way to stay in business.

Of course empowering your employees in this way means that you must hire people with good judgement, train them well and cultivate an environment where they want to do what is in the company's best interests. They will need to have empathy to understand what the customer is going through, and they need to be able to think creatively in order to come up with the best possible solution. These are the kind of employees who will ensure that customers who have encountered a problem become your strongest advocates.

REPEAT BUSINESS CHALLENGE

If you don't already have something in place, develop a system that empowers your employees to handle the vast majority of customer complaints. It can be a tiered level depending on the position. Train them to use this system, and then review on a regular basis. Be sure to reward demonstrations of excellent management skills.

ACCOUNTABILITY

In April 2014, CNN reported that at least 40 veterans of the United States armed services had died while waiting for health care at a single facility. Within weeks, an internal audit revealed that nationwide, over 120,000 veterans had waited for months or had never received proper health care for a myriad of conditions. High ranking officials resigned in disgrace, Congress rushed to pass legislation to reform the Veterans' Health Administration, and the nation watched in horror.

The cause of the terrible scandal was ultimately determined to be the lack of accountability for those in charge of the veterans' care. The leaders were theoretically evaluated on how quickly the veterans were served and the quality of care they received, but the relevant evaluation forms could be faked easily. Because veterans had no choice but to be served at these facilities, the abuses and deceit went unnoticed for far too long.

When there is no accountability in a workplace for a significant period of time, most employees not only allow the quality of their work to decline, but they also refuse to take responsibility for what they do or don't do. This tendency can show up in many different ways: by hiding (or attempting to hide) their mistakes, by blaming others, or by simply trying to avoid any significant punishment or consequences for their actions. Over time, these problems become systemic and begin affecting the morale and performance of even the most dedicated employees with the highest personal standards. After all, why should one person work hard to do a good job when someone else does a lousy job and never faces any consequences?

In a perfect world everyone would hold themselves to a high standard even when no one is watching. And when you cultivate the right workplace environment that is often what happens. But there are always people who will do only what they are required to do, and even the best employee can have an off day when it is tempting to do a less than perfect job.

Accountability often sounds like a negative word, but it is really a gift when provided in a respectful, consistent way. Accountability calls us to be our best selves on a regular basis, and prevents us from succumbing to the temptation of being less than we can be. Think about the role accountability plays for many people trying to lose weight. They want to be healthier and improve their appearance, but sometimes that donut or pizza is just too tempting. But the knowledge that they will go to their weight loss center to be weighed is often enough to motivate them to resist in that moment of weakness.

In the same way, a healthy culture of accountability at work can bring out the best in employees. When they are tired or challenged in other ways and tempted to give less than perfect service, the knowledge that someone is checking up on them can be the incentive they need to go the extra mile.

REPEAT BUSINESS CHALLENGE

Instead of catching people doing something wrong, catch them doing something right, and make sure to reward them for their behavior. Accountability is one of the top attributes a person can have in the professional as well as personal world. Accountability is taking responsibility when things go wrong, which they inevitably will. You want to make sure you have the best people in place to handle the situation.

WHAT YOUR EMPLOYEES NEED TO PROVIDE
MORE THAN PERFECT CUSTOMER SERVICE

A PROACTIVE BUT FLEXIBLE APPROACH

We've already discussed why your customers want proactive communication (see #13). Yet most businesses still offer customer service that is primarily reactive. They respond when a customer has a question or a complaint, but otherwise they assume that everything is fine.

Unfortunately, this kind of approach ends up costing your company time and money, while leaving you very vulnerable to competitors who are willing to serve your customers proactively. Writing in *Forbes*, Adrian Swinscoe cites research by Enkata which demonstrates that "a proactive customer service strategy can

1. Reduce inbound customer service call volumes by between 20 to 30 percent over a 12 month period;
2. Lower call center operating costs by as much as 25 percent;

3. Has a positive effect on customer retention, boosting it by 3 to 5 percent."

In short, if you and your employees can anticipate your customers' needs and address them proactively, you'll receive fewer complaints and questions. So it's pretty safe to say that a well-trained employee is a proactive employee who will see potential problems and solve them before they affect the customer significantly. Proactive employees do things like salt the walkway before the snow starts, make sure the company's website and social media accounts stay appropriately updated, and check on the areas they are responsible for without being constantly reminded to do so.

The key to offering proactive service is to ensure that all your employees know what the more than perfect customer experience should be. When they know what the ideal is supposed to look like, they can recognize and correct mistakes or discrepancies before they become an issue. In the end, this approach saves everyone time and energy.

Of course there is no way to anticipate every possible problem, so your employees also need the ability to think on their feet. This comes more naturally to some than others. The skill that enables people to pivot from one approach to the next is called cognitive flexibility. Cognitive flexibility allows us to "switch gears" when needed, whether that means taking a fresh approach when you're stuck on a math problem or trying a new strategy to resolve an issue for a customer when the first attempt doesn't work.

For employees who struggle with this skill, try role playing scenarios during your training exercises to ensure that they know how to handle a complaining customer, a confused customer, and a distressed customer. (Role playing is fine, but draw the line at costumes. Unless it's Batman, of course.) These exercises help employees feel prepared instead of shell shocked when these situations inevitably arise, and they can actually be a lot of fun.

Of course once an employee has done a great job coming up with a solution on the fly, you don't want to reinvent the wheel each time that problem surfaces. Most companies find it beneficial to develop a "solutions manual" for each department. Each time a new problem occurs, the employee who encountered it records the problem and the solution in a binder (or in an online shared document). The entire staff is then briefed on the solution at the next regular meeting or training session. When appropriate, the employee who came up with the solution can be rewarded. This way the entire staff can benefit from their collective, not just individual, experiences.

REPEAT BUSINESS CHALLENGE

Have a proactive but flexible approach with your team. Encourage your team to share ideas on how to move the company forward and improve on customer service objectives. When you make employees feel like part of the solution, they will instinctively be more inclined to proactively address a problem.

A POSITIVE ATTITUDE

The most brilliant, highly skilled, attractive and experienced employee can be rendered useless or even harmful to your business by a negative attitude. On the other hand, an employee who may lack certain skills or abilities can still be a tremendous asset to your company if he or she consistently maintains a positive attitude. That is why attitude is one of the most important qualities to assess during the interview and hiring process.

Countless books have been written about the power and importance of a positive attitude. When it comes to serving customers, a positive attitude is more than just optimism or "seeing the glass half full." A positive attitude is the determination to make the best of every situation and demonstrate superior work. Ultimately, a positive attitude conveys gratitude and care, even in the face of challenges.

It isn't hard to imagine how important a positive attitude is to providing excellent customer service. Just smiling and offering a cheerful greeting can really brighten your customers' day and make them want to spend more time in your establishment. And of course a negative attitude can have exactly the opposite effect.

But perhaps the most important thing to know about attitudes is that they are contagious. That's why it is so important to be sure that your employees are committed to maintaining a positive attitude at work: one bad attitude can spread shockingly quickly and poison countless interactions between coworkers and with customers.

In her December 2015 Harvard Business Review article *It's Better to Avoid a Toxic Employee than Hire a Superstar* Nicole Torres explains the damage that toxic employees do to the company, "[A study] compared the cost of a toxic worker with the value of a superstar, which they define as a worker who is so productive that a firm would have to hire additional people or pay current employees more just to achieve the same output. They calculated that avoiding a toxic employee can save a company more than twice as much as bringing on a star performer."

All this demonstrates that attitudes do indeed spread from one person to another. Just like you would rather a sick employee stay home than come to work and give everyone else their virus, you are better off without the employee with a bad attitude, even if that person seems to be a highly productive member of the team in other ways. Also make sure you compliment and publicly affirm employees who consistently demonstrate positive attitudes, even in the face of challenges. Sometimes it is easy to take positive people for granted, but acknowledging their contribution can encourage others to follow their example.

Ultimately, positive attitudes start at the top with you, the leader. If you want your employees to have positive attitudes, you must be sure to demonstrate your own consistently. If you fail to be positive in a moment of weakness, acknowledge it to your staff and apologize.

No one is perfect, but your willingness to admit falling short will serve to emphasize the importance of this principle.

REPEAT BUSINESS CHALLENGE

Stress the importance of a positive attitude from the interview process. Company culture is a main factor in employee engagement and satisfaction. Maintain a positive attitude and encourage others to do the same with a reward system in place for positive leadership.

A DESIRE TO LEARN

Jason and Kevin were hired at a telecommunications firm the same year, both in the same department. Kevin began at a higher salary, because he had a bachelor's degree, while Jason just had an associate's with the appropriate certifications. Five years later, however, Jason was managing the entire department, while Kevin still held the same position he had been hired for. What happened?

Both men were hard working, but Jason was an avid learner. He attended every optional training the company offered, studied on the weekends, and asked his supervisors questions whenever he had the opportunity. Soon he had demonstrated that he was ready for more responsibility. Kevin was content to stay where he was and was not interested in spending any extra time at the office.

Remember, giving more than perfect customer service requires employees who enjoy challenges and are looking for opportunities to learn and grow. Anyone can do things perfectly when the task is easy, but who can make customers smile when a hailstorm or a manufacturer error has thrown a wrench in their experience? That's the real test. Some people shut down in these kinds of situations, while others rise to the occasion and shine. Employees who love to learn are the ones who are much more likely to step up and find a solution.

Jason's professional advancement was driven by much more than just ambition. He was genuinely curious and wanted to grow. Of course you need to hire employees that possess a level of competency that ensures their performance will meet your standards from day one. However, once you have established that a candidate can meet those standards, you are probably better off hiring someone that is eager to learn rather than someone who is complacent, even if he or she seems more qualified in other ways.

Ultimately, both Jason and Kevin were good employees who did their jobs well. And there really isn't anything wrong with Kevin's contentment with his job and desire to spend any extra time he has on his hobbies or with his family. But if you do not create a culture that encourages professional development and offers continual opportunities to improve and advance, you will lose employees like Jason. They will become bored or feel like there is no room for growth in your company.

Remember, you want your employees to take pride in their work, and creating a culture for continual education is a vital part of making that happen. Enthusiastic and ambitious employees should feel challenged in a positive way. They should feel they can gain new skills and take on increasing responsibility while they are working for you. Solid employees like Kevin can still be great assets, but be on the lookout for people like Jason who are excited to rise to the top.

REPEAT BUSINESS CHALLENGE

Encourage learning within your company and give incentives for those who take the time and make the effort to expand their knowledge and skill sets. Offer monthly training if possible and encourage company leaders to implement professional development strategies within their teams.

THE ABILITY TO SET REASONABLE AND CLEAR CUSTOMER EXPECTATIONS

As we've already covered extensively, customer satisfaction is directly related to how closely an outcome matches initial expectations. If you are expecting a downpour on your hike, you may be delighted with only a light drizzle. But if you were expecting sunshine, you may be sorely disappointed with the same weather. So it is very important that both you and your employees know how to set clear and realistic expectations for your customers. A wonderful—even a more than perfect—customer experience can become disappointing if the initial expectation is too high.

Of course many people make unrealistic promises to try to hook a new customer or close a sale. This only sets the customer up for disappointment in the long term. Furthermore, when something goes wrong, it can be very tempting to make unrealistic promises to the customer to alleviate the immediate tension. For example, if the kitchen messes up an order in a restaurant, the server may be tempted to say, "I am so sorry! I told the kitchen about the mistake and I'll have your order out to you in five minutes!"

This kind of promise might help for a moment, because it is what the customer wants to hear. But if the order is a well-done burger, or if it is a busy Saturday night in the restaurant, the promise of five minutes may not be realistic, even if the kitchen rushes as fast as it can. The server in this situation may ultimately have to offer another apology, if the order takes eight minutes instead of five.

If the server had promised the new meal in ten minutes from the beginning—a little more realistic—the customer might have been initially impatient but wouldn't have had to be disappointed for a second time. If the server was unsure of the time it would take, she might have promised something along the lines of "We will get that out to you as soon as possible" or a similar statement that gave her a little more flexibility.

Setting clear expectations means going above and beyond simply telling the customer the truth. It also means ensuring that the customer understands what you are communicating to avoid misunderstandings in the future. This is the opposite of all those customer agreements that are written in tiny print to ensure that no one ever reads them. The goal of those companies is to get customers to agree to something they don't understand. Then if there is a problem, they can always point back to the fine print to prove that the customer should have known better. This kind of practice might work for major credit card companies and virtually everyone in Washington DC, but it won't lead to repeat customers for your business.

Setting clear and realistic expectations requires setting aside the emotionally easier choice of promising the customer something huge now, for the long term goal of making the customer want to come back. The old adage that it is better to undersell and over-perform definitely holds true for anyone who wants to cultivate loyal customers. Remind your employees that customers want to be dealt with honestly (see #22) and that setting clear and realistic expectations now will lead to greater customer satisfaction in the long run.

REPEAT BUSINESS CHALLENGE

Roleplaying can be an inventive way to ensure your team is using the "undersell and over-perform" method of communication. Encourage your team to think of ways to implement these methods on the spot when dealing with customers. Possess the ability to set reasonable and clear customer expectations.

THE DESIRE TO CONNECT PERSONALLY WITH CUSTOMERS

"Okay, will that be all, Mr. Cooper?" Katie asked politely from her teller's window at the bank. There was only an hour until closing, and she was eager to prepare for the weekend ahead.

"Umm, I guess so," the gentleman replied. He was clearly past retirement age and had been asking about buying savings bonds for his grandchildren. Katie had answered all his questions, but he still hadn't made a final decision.

"Okay, then! Have a good weekend," Katie said, again very courteously. The gentleman looked down at his shoes and shuffled out of the bank to his car.

Almost all of us describe ourselves as "great with people," but what does this really mean? Being polite and displaying decent manners are really the minimum requirements for professional behavior. On the surface, there was nothing wrong with how Katie served Mr. Cooper at her window. However—although she did everything her job description required—she really didn't help him with what he needed. If Katie had been interested in connecting personally with him, she probably could have figured out what was confusing or worrying him and helped him come to a decision. What someone like Katie needs, and what you want in your employees, is a willingness and desire to form a relationship—albeit a professional one—with the people who buy from the company.

According to a study by Mori, customers who have an emotional connection with your business are at least three times more likely to recommend you to their friends and family members than customers who haven't connected with any of your employees. Connected customers are also three times more likely to buy from you repeatedly, are less likely to shop around the next time they are buying what you sell and are more likely to buy from you even if they find a cheaper competitor.

There are very simple ways to connect with your customers. You can start by learning your customers' names and then learning something significant, interesting or unusual about each of them. Katie already knew Mr. Cooper's name and that he had grandchildren. What if she had taken the time to ask him about his grandchildren's ages and interests? Depending on your industry, you may want to keep this information filed somewhere, or even use a customer relationship management (CRM) software program to keep all the relevant facts at your fingertips.

Forming meaningful connections will come very naturally to some of your employees, but others will need to be trained more extensively. Even people who are not naturally social can learn to say the right things, ask the right questions and offer the right non-verbal cues in order to connect effectively. I have had a great deal of success teaching people who were initially very awkward to get comfortable learning more about and bonding with those they serve.

Although you want your company's culture of customer service to be strengthened by positive reinforcement by rewarding the right behaviors, there will inevitably be times when you have to discipline or even fire employees for violating your values. The question you should ask when there is an issue is to what degree the problem was due to lack of training, to what degree it was due to lack of maturity or self-control and to what degree was the violation deliberate. An employee who was unintentionally rude or brisk and is truly sorry can probably be trained not to make the same mistake again. Newer or younger employees may still be learning how to handle themselves professionally in the face of fatigue, stress or boredom.

If any employee has a particularly problematic temper or is intentionally violating the rules and procedures you have laid down, then it may be time to let that person go. You must protect your culture of excellent customer service and you cannot allow a few bad apples to ruin it. The good news is that once you have established this kind of environment, connecting with customers becomes the norm.

REPEAT BUSINESS CHALLENGE

Evaluate how you are investing in your customers. Do you have a system in place to remember birthdays, special events or requests? Making a small effort will take you a long way with your customers in the lifetime of your business relationship. Go above and beyond the call of duty and show each customer they are important.

SECTION IV

WHAT YOU NEED TO LEAD A COMPANY THAT GIVES MORE THAN PERFECT SERVICE

Now that you know what your employees need to provide more than perfect service, it is time to discuss what you need in order to lead them and ensure they remain equipped to do their jobs. As a 2008 article in Harvard Business Review put it, "Real change has to come from the top…When the rank and file see that their leaders–from their direct supervisors to those in the executive suite–are committed to keeping the customer in their sights, they are more likely to strive for the same focus."

Remember that the environment you create at work will determine the kind of service your company offers its clients and customers. You cannot treat your employees harshly or indifferently and expect them to turn on a dime and be courteous and warm to the customers they serve. The way you conduct yourself will set the standard for how your employees will behave and how they will treat others.

But the responsibilities of leadership mean that you also need to take care of yourself. You cannot run yourself ragged and expect to give your employees the leadership that they need. However, the better you take care of yourself, the more you will see the spillover effect in your company. When you are healthier—physically, emotionally, intellectually—you will be better able to offer specific advice and guidance. Your energy, enthusiasm and creativity will spread to those around you.

WHAT YOU NEED TO LEAD A COMPANY THAT GIVES
MORE THAN PERFECT SERVICE

STRONG ROLE MODELS

Growing up in New England, I loved watching the Boston Celtics play basketball. The undisputed NBA greats of that era were men like Kareem Abdul-Jabbar and Dr. J. But my favorite player was John Havlicek, the Celtics guard who was an irreplaceable part of eight NBA championships during my childhood. If ESPN highlights had existed back then, he might not have made the reel that often. Rather than sensational dunks, his nightly contributions were things like solid, versatile defense, and great fundamentals in passing and shooting. He was a brilliant athlete, but he also seemed unwilling to be outworked, ensuring night after night that he was in better shape than almost any of his opponents.

Watching Havlicek (and later, the great Larry Bird) inspired me to work hard at what I did as well. I knew I would never be a professional basketball player, but I realized I could put my heart and soul into whatever I did, just like my heroes. I didn't realize it at the time, but I think a huge reason I looked up to these men was that they were like superstar versions of my own dad. He didn't have a college degree, but he worked hard every day to ensure our family had everything we needed. He was a simple man who just treated people right, and in turn, was deeply respected by all his coworkers, family members and friends.

Who do you look up to and why? There is a limit to what we can learn from written lessons and abstract theories. Particularly when it comes to character, we learn much better from seeing those principles and ideals lived out in everyday life. And those we admire end up shaping who we become.

Every leader needs strong role models. Of course some of these will be people who have achieved or surpassed your professional goals. Earlier in my career, I was deeply influenced by a coworker named Lesley, whose prim British accent and impeccable attire never prevented her from laboring physically to complete a task, whether it was moving heavy equipment or putting together large pieces of furniture. She showed me that any leader—from the CEO down—was not above any task, and that they should be willing to do anything they asked their employees to do.

Many of your role models, however, may simply be people who exhibit qualities you admire deeply and desire to see within yourself. Such examples are even more important as our popular culture tends to dismiss or even celebrate behavior that is outrageous, rude or even what would have at one time been called shameful. (Little known fact: "Shameful" is an old Greek word, meaning "Kardashian.") A huge part of leading a company that gives more than perfect service is reclaiming what many may see as "old-fashioned" manners, and making them normal again. (We'll talk about this more a little later.)

Writing in Psychology Today, Dr. Susan Krauss Whitbourne discusses a 2013 Pennsylvania State University study that sought to determine the importance of adult role models in the lives and performance of business leaders. The study found "that having adult role models, then, directly impacts not only how you [as a leader] perceive yourself but, just as importantly, how others perceive you." She goes on to explain that if the people you look up to have questionable ethics—even if they are very successful—you may soon find yourself compromising your own standards. This is true, according to Whitbourne, regardless of how high your personal standards were previously.

Take the time to think about who your role models are. If you can't think of anyone admirable on the list, it may be time to seek out new ones.

REPEAT BUSINESS CHALLENGE

Encourage your team to seek out and discuss what they learn from strong role models. Make sure management is held to a high standard of leadership that makes them a role model to other employees, and recognize those who go out of their way to implement inspiring behavior.

RESPECT FOR THE POWER OF CHOICE

Every day we make hundreds of choices that range in nature from mundane—what we will have for breakfast and wear to work—to critical. Almost all of us recognize that our choices have consequences, both good and bad, intended and unintended. But not everyone views these choices the same way. Some—whether they realize it or not—see their choices as relatively inconsequential. They view their lives as something that happens to them, not as something they help to create.

The rest of us see choices as central to the direction and quality of our lives. We understand that circumstances may seem unfair at times, but we focus on what we can control. As we grow and mature, we believe that if we learn to make wiser choices, our lives will turn out infinitely better than if we simply treat our choices lightly.

One of the defining qualities of a good leader is understanding that our choices affect more than just ourselves. Thus leaders must be people who respect the power of choice and take each daily decision seriously. We must take the time to think through our choices without becoming indecisive or bogged down in the minutiae.

The ability to take full responsibility for our choices is associated with autonomy. Autonomy is a frequently discussed term in politics, often referring to the right or capacity of a nation or a group to govern itself. But the concept also applies to individuals; to be truly free and happy, we must have a sense that we are making our choices in an informed and reasonable manner, free from coercion or compulsion.

How does this apply to leading an organization that offers superior customer service? Anyone who leads this kind of organization must have a strong sense of autonomy. Without it, we are doomed to make excuses for poor performance. Just as we want our employees to have a sense that they determine the quality of their work, we must demonstrate this first by example.

Of course there will always be factors that deeply affect your company and your decisions—or even your ability to do your job—that are beyond your control. These can include things like personal medical emergencies, changes in your industry, actions of competitors or even shifts in the local or national economy. Do your best to identify these factors and determine the best course of action. This could include anything from bringing a problem to the attention of your superiors, to seeking counsel from a business adviser or mentor. But if there is truly nothing you can do, accept what you cannot change and focus on what you can.

It is very easy to see how people born into extraordinarily challenging or particularly privileged circumstances might see life in fatalistic terms. After all, someone in abject poverty has to work extremely hard to get out and someone with extravagant wealth will probably not lose it all. But the overwhelming majority of us are born somewhere in between, and we have much more power over where life takes us than we recognize. Demonstrate this daily to your employees and watch them follow your example.

REPEAT BUSINESS CHALLENGE

Being autonomous is all about trust. Set up a reward system for those employees who have displayed the skill and character to make great choices for the company.

HIGH STANDARDS

Tammy stared at the draft of the memo in front of her that was covered with red marks. Her manager Carol had taken her infamous red pen to the document and marked all sorts of changes to what Tammy had written. Tammy sighed as she read it over for a second time and made the changes. Most of the items Carol had marked were not errors, but just word choices that she didn't seem to like. Tammy checked her revisions several more times and sent the file back to Carol.

Carol was notorious for making multitudes of corrections to anything that made it to her inbox. She seemed to find fault in everything whether it was a memo, copy for the website or the way the flowers looked in the foyer. Everyone dreaded sending things to her for approval, because they knew they were bound to get an earful.

The next day, Tammy received the second draft of her memo back from Carol. She laughed. Carol had marked it up again, this time reversing some of the changes that she had made to it the first time. Without realizing it, Carol had "corrected" some of her own corrections!

Almost all of us have had a boss or a supervisor like Carol; someone who seems to take pleasure in finding mistakes and offering corrections or even rebukes to employees. But you don't have to be hyper-critical of others in order to have high standards. In fact, when you are a real leader, all the standards for your business start with you.

High standards begin with things like your own personal appearance, your commitment to being on time and doing an excellent job with all of your own duties. This sets a clear example for your employees and shows that you are not asking them to do anything that you are not willing to do yourself. When you fail to live up to your own standards (and if they are high, you will sometimes fail) you acknowledge the failure and apologize to anyone who may have been affected.

Unfortunately, people who are hyper-critical—like Carol—often make excuses for any breaches in their own performance or fail to acknowledge them at all. This is because their criticism of others is driven not by truly high standards, but by a desire to make others feel inferior in order to compensate for their own insecurity. Acknowledging your own shortcomings shows that you believe the standard applies to you as well as to everyone else.

To have high standards, you must have a very clear understanding of what your job entails and what it looks like when you have done it correctly. For leaders to have high standards, they must understand this for all the jobs of the people who report to them. And for individuals to successfully demonstrate high standards on a consistent basis, they must be intrinsically motivated to do so.

There are two basics types of behavioral motivators: intrinsic and extrinsic. Extrinsic motivators are—as their name suggests—external rewards. These include things like money, prestige and influence that we gain by making certain decisions. Of course all of us work to some extent for the money and prestige, but some people are motivated almost exclusively by these kinds of benefits.

Intrinsic motivators come from deep inside us. They include things like pride in a job well done, a desire to learn new things, and so on. Writing in *Forbes*, Heidi Grant Halvorson observes of intrinsic motivation, "When people are intrinsically motivated, they enjoy what they are doing more, and find it more interesting. They feel more creative, and process information more deeply. They persist more in the face of difficulty. They perform better. Intrinsic motivation is awesome in its power to get and keep us going."

When we truly possess high personal standards for our work, our own internal standards will exceed those of the customer or the manager. Our desire to meet those standards will come from deep within us. That kind of motivation is contagious. When your employees see that you won't accept mediocre work for yourself, they will not want to accept it either.

REPEAT BUSINESS CHALLENGE

Ask your employees to explore what truly motivates them. This will offer incredible insight on how they process the work they are doing and how they are best rewarded. Encourage constructive criticism when reviewing tasks. Everyone wants to feel respected in the role that they play.

DETERMINATION

The phrase "Find a way or make one," has been attributed to a number of historical figures including Carthaginian General Hannibal—who, according to legend, said it before he famously led an army over the Swiss Alps by elephant—and the English poet Philip Sidney. Whoever actually said it, the meaning is clear. Don't let the challenges facing you prevent you from accomplishing your goal. Discover a path to your objective, or forge a new one.

During my time as a cruise director, a newlywed couple arrived on board one of our ships without the suitcase that contained their evening gowns and tuxedos for the formal dinners onboard. Of course it wasn't our fault the airline lost their luggage, but our determined crew went to work on the problem. Within three hours the stateroom attendant was able to secure a tuxedo and a beautiful gown in their sizes, and their missing suitcase was successfully recovered at the first port of call. Needless to say, they were not only pleased, but are now loyal customers of the cruise line.

The idea of determination is often misused in the workplace. It becomes an excuse for ruthless behavior, coldblooded ambition or doing whatever it takes to get ahead. But that is not what real determination is. The determined leader is one who is committed to whatever ethical course of action will lead the group—whether it's a department, a task force or an entire company—to its collective goal. In short, the determined leader is the leader devoted to getting the job done.

In her book *Grit: The Power of Passion and Perseverance*, psychologist and researcher Dr. Angela Duckworth explains that determination or "grit" is far more important than IQ, standardized test scores and many other measures when it comes to predicting an individual's long-term success. And the good news is that, while some aspects of grit may be inborn, it can also be learned and developed. Duckworth explained to the New York Times that an important key to cultivating grit is to develop genuine interest in the task at hand:

> *"You cannot will yourself to be interested in something you're not interested in. But you can actively discover and deepen your interest. So once you've fostered an interest, then, and only then, can you do the kind of difficult, effortful and sometimes frustrating practice that truly makes you better. Another thing is really maintaining a sense of hope or resilience, even when there are setbacks."*

It follows then that an important key to developing the kind of determination and perseverance necessary to provide more than perfect customer service in a less than perfect world is to develop a genuine interest in your employees and customers. (We'll talk about this more in #47.) The more you care about your customers and employees on a personal level, the easier it will be to do whatever it takes to give them what they need.

When a leader lacks resolve, it is very difficult to inspire others to follow. But determination, like many other qualities, can be contagious. When your employees know that you are fully committed to giving your customers the best, they will be far more excited to commit to it as well.

REPEAT BUSINESS CHALLENGE

Sit down with your team and discuss what they are most passionate about regarding the services you provide. Take this knowledge and determine how to create a plan to use this passion and determination to improve other areas of your business.

THREE KEY ATTRIBUTES: RESPECT, RESPONSIBILITY AND RELIABILITY

Leaders should be both respectful and respected. The old saying that you have to give respect to get it is particularly true of anyone who leads others: if you don't treat your followers with respect, they will not respect you back. Respect is something you must earn daily from those around you by the way you conduct yourself, but it is also something that you must give freely.

Part of being a respectful leader is staying away from company gossip. Gossip can take the form of repeating rumors about the company—someone's promotion, downsizing, opening up a new location, and so on—or it can involve the personal lives of employees. The first type of gossip causes confusion, the second type can be incredibly toxic to workplace relationships.

Although it can be very tempting to listen to the silly or even sordid details of other people's lives, you must determine to remain above that kind of discourse. No matter how juicy, no matter how funny, no matter how YouTube worthy, the fact remains: Gossip directly undermines trust. If you entertain people's whisperings about others, they will ultimately lose respect for you. Even if they seem to enjoy it, they will know that you might be gossiping about them next time. Ultimately, gossip destroys teamwork and undermines productivity.

Effective leaders also take responsibility for their own words and actions and for the performance of those they lead. This responsibility works itself out in many ways. In day to day interactions, responsible leaders don't look for ways to find fault in others. Instead, when something isn't going well, they look at themselves and consider what they could be doing differently to bring about a different outcome. Ultimately, responsible leaders make sure that everyone on their team has the training and resources they need to do their jobs well.

There are several ways leaders may subconsciously avoid their responsibilities. They may delay making an important decision on the pretext that they are too busy. They may reverse a decision without acknowledging or explaining what they are doing to the people the decision affects. They may fail to communicate important information because doing so makes them uncomfortable or risks upsetting others. Even micromanaging one's employees can be a form of avoiding the responsibility to train, empower and delegate.

And of course the most common way leaders avoid responsibility is by blaming others for things that have gone wrong, especially when offering explanations to their superiors. Fortunately, when you consistently take responsibility for your words and actions, you can expect others to follow suit. Leaders who know that the buck stops with them will find that their employees take the same attitude toward their jobs.

Leaders should be known for their reliability. This means that people trust you to keep your word. When people ask you to do something, they fully expect that you will do it. If you don't, they know that extreme circumstances must have arisen and they know you will explain what happened.

Being reliable doesn't mean that you always do exactly what you say you will do. After all, we get caught in traffic jams, catch a cold or encounter some circumstance beyond our control which prevents us from keeping our word. However, if you acknowledge your failure to fulfill your promise and apologize, it shows the person you let down that you still take your promise seriously.

Reliability is also associated with consistent behavior. All of us get emotional at times, and sometimes it can be tempting to act on a sudden, strong feeling. But this is rarely a good idea. There are simple steps you can take to prevent yourself from behaving impulsively and then regretting it later. For example, never send an email when you are feeling upset, angry or stressed out. Write it, save it as a draft and revisit it the next day. Same thing with phone calls and personal conversations: unless the situation is absolutely urgent, wait until you feel calm and collected before you deal with it.

At the heart of being able to be reliable is self-awareness and maturity. You may be irritable when you are hungry or tired; know this about yourself and take the appropriate steps to make sure you are well rested and fed. If you sense yourself getting distracted, take the time to refocus. Good leaders are not perfect, but they know themselves well enough to take steps to compensate for their weaknesses.

REPEAT BUSINESS CHALLENGE

Evaluate yourself and your team to discover if you are implementing the true qualities of leadership. Reward your team members who take responsibility for their actions in order to encourage accountability.

THREE IMPORTANT VALUES: EMPATHY, GRATITUDE AND COMPASSION

We've already discussed how important empathy is as a value for employees, so it should be no surprise that it is important for you as a leader as well. Empathetic leaders are not only able to connect better with their employees; they are also able to demonstrate how to connect empathetically with customers. When your employees feel like you truly understand and care about what they are going through, they are much better able to show similar care for others.

Gratitude doesn't just make you a more pleasant person to be around. Multiple studies indicate it is good for your mental health as well. Writing in Psychology Today, author Amy Morin explains the psychological benefits of gratitude: "Gratitude reduces a multitude of toxic emotions, from envy and resentment to frustration and regret.

Robert Emmons, a leading gratitude researcher, has conducted multiple studies on the link between gratitude and well-being. His research confirms that gratitude effectively increases happiness and reduces depression."

Morin also explains that gratitude leads to higher quality sleep, better relationships and even better physical health. As a leader, gratitude sets a positive tone for everything that happens. But it's important to go beyond just "feeling" grateful. To get the maximum benefit from gratitude, you actually need to express it to others. Amazingly, according to several studies including a 2012 series published in the Journal of Personality and Social Psychology, expressing genuine thanks benefits both the giver and the receiver.

Compassion can be thought of as a more engaged form of empathy; some people explain compassion for the suffering as actually suffering with them, while focusing on alleviating their pain. Compassion is activated when we care about someone else's struggles as much we care about our own. In her Harvard Business Review article *Why Compassion is a Better Managerial Tactic than Toughness*, Emma Seppala explains why compassion may be a better response to unintentional employee mistakes:

> *"In particular, a study by Jonathan Haidt of New York University shows that the more employees look up to their leaders and are moved by their compassion or kindness (a state he terms elevation), the more loyal they become to him or her. So if you are more compassionate to your employee, not only will he or she be more loyal to you, but anyone else who has witnessed your behavior may also experience elevation and feel more devoted to you."*

Compassion doesn't mean that you lower your standards or overlook mistakes; it simply means that you respond to your employees as human beings in the same way you would want your superior to respond to you. Compassion also motivates you to want to give back to those around you—as well as to those less fortunate than you—especially as you enjoy greater success. When your entire team is motivated by compassion, community service activities (like those discussed in #6) quickly become second nature.

REPEAT BUSINESS CHALLENGE

Showing that you care for your employees and customers is essential to long-term success. How are you connecting to your team members? Are you displaying compassion to others who are going through a hard time? Get to know your team and customers on a personal level and exhibit compassion in an effort to understand and resolve an issue they have.

A STRONG PLAN

All leaders need to be able to formulate a strong plan, and leaders who value customer service are no exception. Part of creating an effective plan is asking the right questions. The primary questions are straightforward: what are we trying to accomplish, how are we going to do it and in what time frame? But there are deeper questions that truly strategic leaders will ask that will greatly increase their chances of success.

Effective leaders ask questions about purpose and priorities during the planning process. For example, if they are planning a specific initiative, they ask questions about why the initiative is important and how it fits into the bigger picture for the company. If they are planning for the entire organization, they ask relevant questions about the industry that they are part of and how their plan fits with those trends or changes.

They also adhere to the old adage, "Plan for the worst and hope for the best" by asking questions about their own inherent biases that may be preventing them from seeing drawbacks to their plan. One of the most effective ways to guard against wishful thinking in planning is to create a "pre-mortem" before moving forward with any major plan. Psychologist and Nobel Prize winner Daniel Kahneman advocates this practice, which was developed by his colleague Gary Klein. Kahneman explains the pre-mortem exercise in his book *Thinking, Fast and Slow*:

> "When the organization has almost come to an important decision but hasn't committed itself, it should gather a group of people knowledgeable about the decision to listen to a brief speech: 'Imagine that we are a year into the future. We implemented the plan as it now exists. The outcome has been a disaster. Please take 5 to 10 minutes to write a brief history of that disaster.'"

Anticipating the potential drawbacks of a certain course of action allows you to account for them and will ultimately make your plan stronger. In the area of customer service, consider every step of the customer experience journey. It can be extremely helpful to conduct research among your customer base—by written surveys, online questionnaires, or one-on-one interviews—to help gauge the likely effectiveness of your plan. Questions should assess customer needs, desires and expectations. You can also gather useful data in this area from your frontline employees who interact with customers on a regular basis.

Lastly, it is extremely important that you evaluate your plan as it is implemented and after it has been in place for a while. Is it having the effect you had hoped it would? Are the results better or worse than expected? Are there factors in play that you did not anticipate?

Remember, it's impossible to anticipate every possible outcome, but it is always possible to correct course.

> **REPEAT BUSINESS CHALLENGE**
>
> Review your short and long-term plans with your team and allow them to be part of the process. Employees who feel they are "brought to the table" in decision making agendas will be far more invested in the goals of your organization.

OPTIMISM

Intel co-founder Robert Noyce called optimism "an essential ingredient of innovation. How else," he asked, "can the individual welcome change over security, adventure over staying in safe places?" And it's true. Progress is impossible without people who truly believe that there are better ways of doing things, that the future is (or at least can be) bright.

Optimism is also an essential ingredient in leadership. No one wants to follow someone who doesn't believe in a positive future. Pessimism can be very tempting on days where nothing seems to be going right. When life is looking bleak, it can feel safer to assume that things will go badly than to risk being wrong or disappointed. Yet capable leaders will find ways to inspire people to hope for and work for the best, even in the most discouraging circumstances.

No one is saying you have to go full James T. Kirk, cheat on the Kobayashi Maru and "not believe in a no-win scenario," (Trekkies will understand) but to lead an organization that gives more than perfect customer service, you must believe that every problem has a solution—or at least an optimal response. Pessimists will always have excuses for why a guest did not receive superior service on a particular occasion, and such excuses can become addictive. As soon as you justify doing a substandard job one time, it becomes easier to do the same thing the next time. Soon you are offering excuses as a matter of habit more than conviction. An optimistic leader will not only figure out the best possible solution in the moment, but also look for ways to improve the team's response in the future.

Writing in *Psychology Today*, Annie Murphy Paul explains why optimism is so important to success in almost anything: "Even an ordinary effort like going on a diet can benefit from a dose of optimism, research finds…Optimism provides a much-needed boost: It convinces us that our weight-loss goal is achievable, it fortifies our resolve to resist temptations such as snacks and desserts, and it persuades us to climb back on the wagon when we've slipped—because, we optimistically believe, those pounds are simply bound to come off."

Optimism should not be mistaken for delusional thinking. There is a difference between making the best of a bad situation and denying that the challenges exist or that they are as serious as they actually are. Most people can quickly tell the difference. Hiding from or avoiding a problem does not inspire confidence in those you lead. But acknowledging a problem and all its potential complications while still retaining a positive outlook can be incredibly powerful.

REPEAT BUSINESS CHALLENGE

Are you exhibiting optimism in the face of adversity? Opening lines of communication about your team's concerns and remaining optimistic about making positive change is both encouraging and instills loyalty. When people know you are looking towards a bright future, you become a leader who is easy to follow and work hard beside.

AVAILABILITY

"They're here!"

The entire kitchen and wait staff rushed to check their stations when they heard Steve's words. A food safety inspection is never a fun ordeal for any restaurant, but everyone knew this new inspector was infamous for being extremely particular. Five star restaurants in the area had been written up for minor infractions, and two establishments had been temporarily closed. Steve, the general manager, had been uncharacteristically on edge all day.

A formidable woman soon arrived with a clip board, and Steve escorted her to each wait station and to every part of the kitchen. The floors had been freshly mopped. The bleach solution for cleaning had been mixed to exactly the right concentration, and the refrigerators and freezers were all registering the correct temperatures.

But true to her reputation, the inspector soon found a problem: the coffee creamers were in the proper container, but the container was not over ice. The wait staff had assumed this wasn't a problem, since the creamers themselves were shelf stable and did not need to be refrigerated. But according to the inspector's interpretation of the rules she was enforcing, they needed to be kept over ice nonetheless.

Steve was furious and embarrassed. Furious because his restaurant was written up for such a minor technicality and embarrassed because he had known this might be an issue but had forgotten to warn the wait staff about it. He spent the rest of the day sulking in his office with the door closed. No one dared go in and disturb him.

To lead an organization that gives more than perfect service, you must be available to your employees, even when you don't feel like dealing with anyone. There are several good reasons for this. You will never be able to effectively monitor the quality of the service your company offers if you do not have a sense of your employees' morale, mood and performance. You will never be able to have your finger on the "pulse" of the company, so to speak, unless you make yourself available to those you employ.

Leaders who shut themselves off from the people who are actually interacting with the customers not only come across as aloof, but they also risk becoming completely out of touch. Even a friendly boss is often perceived as hostile if he or she does not welcome spontaneous interactions with employees. Of course there may be times that you simply must be left alone in order to do your job. But other than extreme circumstances, you will need an open door policy if you want to provide more than perfect customer service on a regular basis.

The most important time you must make sure you are reachable is if you have made a mistake or if there has been some sort of interpersonal conflict you need to mediate. Instead of hiding in his office, Steve should have called everyone together after the inspector had left and explained what happened. He should have taken full responsibility for not warning the wait staff and invited anyone with any questions to see him personally. This would have resolved the situation and ensured a better outcome in the future. Instead, he alienated his employees and made a bad situation worse.

You can't lead if you aren't there. And if your office door is closed, you may be perceived as "away," even if you are physically around. Open the door, and give your employees the full benefit of your fully engaged presence.

REPEAT BUSINESS CHALLENGE

Encourage an open door policy in your office. It may initially seem difficult setting time aside every day to handle questions and concerns, but having an open door policy and open communication with your employees lets them know their opinions are valued and respected.

A GOOD SENSE OF HUMOR

President Dwight Eisenhower observed, "A sense of humor is part of the art of leadership, of getting along with people, of getting things done." Eisenhower held the highest office in the land at a time when there seemed to be little to laugh about. The Allies had just won World War II, but the Cold War was heating up quickly. Yet Eisenhower was known both for his sense of humor and his relaxed demeanor that put everyone around him at ease. Although dismissed by some of his contemporaries as an intellectual lightweight, most biographers now agree that Eisenhower was much smarter and harder working than he let on. (He was also well known in Washington circles for having the best Groucho Marx impression in DC.)

Most of us will never be under as much pressure at work as President Eisenhower was, but all of us can take a page out of his book and use humor to lighten the mood. Many times, as a cruise director I was challenged with the unenviable task of breaking bad news to the passengers, most often due to weather that was beyond our control.

But I repeatedly found that a few well timed jokes could break the ice and help our customers see the bright side of the situation.

A good sense of humor reveals to your employees that you don't take yourself too seriously. It puts them at ease and helps them feel comfortable being themselves and opening up to you. In fact, a 2012 study by the Bell Leadership Institute in Chapel Hill, North Carolina, found that humor gave leaders a distinct advantage over the less humorous counterparts. Institute founder Dr. Gerald D. Bell explained, "Humor is a vital tool of leadership…Those who can combine a strong work ethic and sense of humor may have the leading edge in their organizations."

Of course not all humor is created equal. Crude or cruel jokes at the expense of others—even if they are not people in your company—are never worth the laughs. On the other hand, self-deprecating humor can be both endearing and motivating for those around you. Being able to laugh at yourself demonstrates both humility and self-assuredness.

Humor also helps you not to overreact to mistakes or unfortunate situations. Sometimes all you can do in the face of an unforeseen challenge is shrug your shoulders, laugh and figure out what to do next. Humor in the workplace also makes life a lot more enjoyable, which will ultimately carry over into everyone's interactions with their customers.

REPEAT BUSINESS CHALLENGE

Do you lead an environment that encourages both hard work and humor? Leading by example is essential for letting others know that it is ok to relax and focus on the problem at hand. Most misunderstandings are due to HOW something was said, not WHAT was said.

A HEALTHY BODY

I t's easy to assume that only athletes have to worry about their physical conditioning in order to do their jobs well. But it turns out our physical health affects our performance no matter what our jobs entail. When we remember that the brain is a physical organ and needs nourishment, exercise and rest, it is easy to understand why a healthy body is vital to a healthy brain.

A study from the Center for Creative Leadership found that business leaders who exercised were significantly more effective than those who didn't. The study observed leaders for over ten years and found that "the exercisers rated significantly higher than their non-exercising peers on overall leadership effectiveness. They also scored higher on specific traits including: inspiring commitment, credibility, leading others, leading by example, energy, resilience and calmness."

Exercise doesn't have to mean three hours a day at the gym (and let's all give a silent word of thanks for that). A 30 minute jog around your neighborhood or on the treadmill a few times a week is much better than doing nothing. Find a form of exercise you like, and stick with it. If you like socializing, join a fitness club or hire a trainer. If you prefer alone time, enjoy a podcast, audio book or some good music.

Of course everyone is busy, and leading a growing company means that it's very easy to skip meals, rely on coffee or energy drinks or grab junk food on the go. These kinds of things aren't a problem if they only happen once in a while, but if they become a habit, you'll soon find that your energy, mood and concentration will suffer.

Stock up on quick but healthy breakfast foods, whether they are fresh fruit, oatmeal, yogurt or smoothies made from healthy ingredients. Keep fruit, nuts, protein bars or other healthy snacks around so you will be less tempted to grab junk because of convenience. If you end up eating at restaurants a lot, make sure to make healthy choices like salad at least most of the time. You may want to consider high quality vitamins or other supplements if you struggle to get enough servings of fruit, vegetables and lean proteins each day.

Lastly, try to get enough sleep. Almost everyone needs at least 7 to 8 hours a day. Of course sometimes circumstances demand that you pull a late night or two, but don't allow that to become the norm. Getting sufficient quantities of high quality sleep is essential to brain function, physical and emotional wellbeing.

These practices might not seem central to leading an organization that gives more than perfect customer service. However, a healthy body really is essential to doing your job well in the long term. Take care of your body now, and you will not regret it later.

REPEAT BUSINESS CHALLENGE

Develop an incentive program for your team members that promotes a healthy lifestyle. Discuss with your team ways that they would like to improve their health, and take steps to implement a program where they will be rewarded for their efforts. Healthy employees are happy employees.

WHAT YOU NEED TO LEAD A COMPANY THAT GIVES
MORE THAN PERFECT SERVICE

GENUINE INTEREST IN YOUR CUSTOMERS AND COWORKERS

Giving more than perfect customer service—and inspiring your employees to do the same—is so much easier when you take a genuine interest in those you serve and those you employ. Anyone can pretend to care during a speech or a one-time meeting, but when you interact daily with the same people, your true feelings become obvious.

Taking a genuine interest in those who work for you is one of the best catalysts for employee engagement. According to a 2015 Gallup Poll, employee disengagement costs the US between 450 and 550 billion dollars per year in lost productivity. This loss can come from employees working more slowly or less enthusiastically than they might otherwise. Most often it shows up as "doing the bare minimum" rather than going above and beyond.

Why are employees disengaged? A 2011 Employee Engagement Survey conducted by Blessing White found that a personal connection to one's manager increased an employee's engagement by 11 points (on average) and led to much higher job satisfaction rates. In short, we all do a better job when we feel cared about.

Employees who feel you take a genuine interest in them will work harder and be happier while they do. The correlation between employee engagement and productivity is completely separate from other job conditions and salary. Remember, you may not always be able to give everyone as large a raise or offer them as many extra perks as you would like. But you have complete control over how much interest you take in your employees' lives, interests and wellbeing. Expressing this interest on a regular basis gives a huge boost to workplace morale and output.

Showing interest in your customers is vital for all the reasons we have already covered. It is essential to offering more than perfect customer service, and it is extremely important to model for your employees and set the tone for all they do. Ultimately, employees who feel the company takes an interest in them will be better able to take an interest in their customers.

There are many ways to demonstrate authentic interest in those you lead and serve. Besides learning their names and important information about them, you can listen attentively on a regular basis. Ask them questions about the things they seem to want to talk about: their jobs, their families, their hobbies or even their pets, while taking care not to be too invasive. Offer genuine, meaningful compliments. And of course you can learn and acknowledge important events in their lives: birthdays, anniversaries, births, graduations, and so on.

Many companies find it helpful to use a database or CRM to keep track of this kind of information. Depending on your industry, you may want to have this information updated monthly, weekly or even daily. Whichever system you use, make sure your employees are properly trained to use it, and that it does not become a burden. Such programs are supposed to make your employees' jobs easier, not more difficult.

REPEAT BUSINESS CHALLENGE

Put in place a system where helpful personal information can be shared and celebrated. Take time to celebrate a birthday or promotion. These acknowledgments cost little to nothing and instill long-term loyalty with your employees.

CULTURAL INTELLIGENCE

Did you know that refusing vodka in Russia is like refusing to shake hands? Or that giving someone a "thumbs up" in Iran is equivalent to extending your middle finger in America? In some countries, people greet each other by shaking hands, in others they do so by bowing; in still others they kiss each other on one cheek or two. (When I was in college, I tried to convince pretty girls that I was from one of those cheek-kissing countries…It didn't work.)

In today's business world, you must be prepared to interact with people from anywhere and everywhere. Different cultures have different concepts of personal space, making eye contact and how to show professionalism and respect. And while it's impossible to memorize the nuances of every single culture on earth, you must be as sensitive as possible to the cultural perspectives of your staff and your customers.

One of the trickiest issues in multicultural environments is how to resolve a problem or complaint. For example, in some countries—including America—it is generally acceptable to resolve a misunderstanding or a logistical conflict by direct communication. If you want to order prime rib at a restaurant, and they have just run out, the server will simply apologize and explain the situation.

In other countries—including places like Japan—this kind of direct refusal is considered unacceptably rude. Rather than tell you there is no prime rib left, the server might appear to agree to your order, but then say something like, "But perhaps you would like the salmon instead?" You must make sure that you and your employees are educated about the customs and expectations of all the people that you serve.

These kinds of challenges might seem difficult to overcome, but the right training can go a long way. Aeroflot—a Russian airline—beat many American airlines in customer service ratings, despite the fact that their employees had to be intentionally trained not to be rude to their customers. According a 2013 article in the New York Times:

> *Gone are the scowls, the cold shoulders and the wordless encounters. Aeroflot introduced training that included compelling candidates to memorize dialogues of pleasantries and reinforcing rules on smiling. Its success in improving service is being taken to heart by other companies in Russia's consumer industries.*

It is well worth your time to read up on the cultural assumptions and customs of the groups of people you are likely to encounter in your professional life. But remember as you do that people are still individuals. Not everyone from a certain country or subculture conforms to all the "standard practices or customs" of that area.

Ultimately, to lead a company that gives more than perfect service to everyone you must develop an intuitive sense of cultural differences and learn to adjust your behavior accordingly. This will enable you not only to lead people from a variety of backgrounds, but also to teach them how to serve people from all over the world.

REPEAT BUSINESS CHALLENGE

Discuss your company culture with your team members and make a commitment to learn about other culture's practices and expectations. Celebrate different company practices and engage your team members to see how you can implement different practices to improve your own organizational experience.

WHAT YOU NEED TO LEAD A COMPANY THAT GIVES
MORE THAN PERFECT SERVICE

A COMMITMENT TO MAKE "UNCOMMON COURTESY" COMMON

So much of superior customer service really just boils down to good manners. Unfortunately, what was once seen as "common courtesy"—the things decent people did all the time—seems to be in short supply these days. Most of this is due to changing social norms; American society became increasingly less formal during the second half of the twentieth century, and that trend appears to be continuing today.

But casual behavior does not have to be impolite. Unfortunately, the fashionable ethic of "authenticity" is frequently confused with rudeness. Some young people in particular seem to think that good manners are somehow inauthentic. If polite behavior does not reflect their mood at any particular moment, they feel showing courtesy is somehow being untrue to themselves.

However, it is important to remember that we are more than just how we feel at any particular moment. There is nothing particularly authentic about acting impulsively on temporary emotions that will change in an hour or two. If rudeness is by nature disrespectful, then courtesy is simply the habit of showing others that we see them as valuable and worthy of respect.

Good manners are also a reflection of how we value ourselves. Dr. Pier Forni, professor at Johns Hopkins University and author of the bestselling book *Choosing Civility: The Twenty-Five Rules of Considerate Conduct,* explains:

> *"Good manners, however, are also something we do for our own sake. They are good for us because as a basic code of relational skills they help us manage our relationships, which are crucial to our well-being and health. Although as adults we may have developed a more sophisticated understanding of manners, chances are that our early bias (that they are for others' sake) still looms large. This may lead us to the wrong conclusion that in the fast-paced, highly competitive and stress-laden environment in which we live, good manners are a luxury we can't afford. I suggest that we balance this view by looking instead at good manners as a precious life-improvement tool for the very people who have them."*

So commit to make uncommon courtesy the norm in your company. Your employees and customers will be glad you did!

REPEAT BUSINESS CHALLENGE

Conduct a workshop on manners. It will be exciting for your team to potentially learn new things as well as address new ways that exceptional service can be implemented with your customers. Investing in the demeanor of your team will only increase your bottom line.

WHAT YOU NEED TO LEAD A COMPANY THAT GIVES
MORE THAN PERFECT SERVICE

COMFORT WITH CHANGE

President John F. Kennedy observed that "Change is the law of life." Most of us have watched the world change in unimaginable ways during our lifetimes, and it is reasonable to expect that such change will continue well into the future. Yet the older we get, the more resistant to change we may become.

To lead an organization that offers more than perfect customer service, you need to be comfortable with change. Ultimately, the peace you have with whatever changes come to your company or your industry will help you and your employees and continue to serve your customers in the best way possible no matter what happens.

We cannot always control what changes come, but we have full control over how we respond to them. Sometimes transformations will occur that require a radical reorganization within your company. These include shifts like mergers, acquisitions, recapitalization (for publically traded companies), as well as rebranding or major identity changes. Often such radical changes are necessary to survive, while other times they are taken as opportunities for growth. They will involve consolidating positions and laying off personnel, reorganizing departments, or other uncomfortable processes. Having peace with such events is vital to effective leadership and maintaining a great customer experience.

Writing in *Harvard Business Review*, Jeanie Daniel Duck explains how changes like reorganizations must be managed with a holistic approach to the organization. "Human resources is not the only support system that must be reevaluated. The organizational mobile has many dimensions—culture, strategy, education, information systems, technology—and they all need to hang together. If the parts of the organizational system are not considered in concert, they will inevitably clash. In the case of process redesign, when the entire mobile is not balanced, reengineering is reduced to a mapping exercise."

It is vital during any kind of change, large or small, that the customer experience remains the focus of your efforts and those of your employees. You must be able to manage any transitions without taking your eye off the people who are keeping you in business. When you do this, your employees will be able to follow your lead.

Customer service itself is changing, and the more effectively companies can anticipate and adapt to these changes, the more they will thrive in the future. Customers have more options than ever, and they expect rapid, personalized responses to their inquiries and complaints. They want to be empowered with more information to make better decisions, but they don't want to spend all day doing research. They appreciate the efficiency of increased automation, but they also want the human touch. The companies that flourish in the decades to come will understand and respond to these needs and desires.

REPEAT BUSINESS CHALLENGE

Change is inevitable, but people will always value respect, loyalty, and great customer service. Discuss with your team how they best handle change, and implement a process that gives your team the communication abilities and confidence to be able to "adjust the sails" when needed. It will only make your sail smoother.

CONCLUSION

Providing service that will make your customers want to do business with you over and over again is not as daunting a task as it may seem. Many of the skills it requires are as old as humanity itself, although they have become increasingly scarce in the digital age. As much as we want everything faster and more convenient than ever before, we still want to connect with real people who really care about us.

At the heart of more than perfect customer service are relationships. The authentic connections we form with those we serve and those we employ become the lifeblood of the companies we lead. Much of leadership is simply forming and nurturing these connections.

So there you have it, 50 tips and strategies you can use today to keep your customers (and employees) coming back tomorrow. Is this the definitive list? Of course not! There are hundreds, even thousands of more tips you can use that will help you grow both personally and professionally.

I have had the unique experience of living with both my customers and co-workers onboard some of the largest and most luxurious cruise ships in the world. We spent 7 days a week, 24 hours a day together in an enclosed floating hotel that traveled all over the world. We had to have policies and procedures in place to make sure they remained loyal and enthusiastic customers. Because of the tips outlined in this book, our customers and employees became our biggest source of advertisement. (Free, advertising, I might add, the best kind!)

Because of these experiences, I have developed a More Than Perfect® Customer Service and Customer Experience program that teaches and trains companies how to deliver a product or service that makes your customers and employees raging brand ambassadors. And isn't that what you want from your hard work, your tireless energy, and your unparalleled dedication?

I would love to hear about your experiences and tips that you have implemented to keep your customers and employees engaged.

Feel free to contact me on Twitter @RealPaulRutter,
at Facebook.com/PaulRutterSpeaks, or at
www.PaulRutterSpeaks.com.

I look forward to connecting with you.
Until then, may all your journeys, both personally
and professionally, be smooth sailing.

www.ingramcontent.com/pod-product-compliance
Lightning Source LLC
Chambersburg PA
CBHW071422180526
45170CB00001B/193